A New Owner's
Guide to
CAVALIER KING
CHARLES SPANIELS

JG-155

Overleaf: Cavalier King Charles Spaniel adult and puppies owned by James and Christine Meager.

Opposite page: A full-grown Cavalier takes a stroll through the yard.

The Publisher wishes to acknowledge the following owners of the dogs in this book: Barbara Aldrich, Cindy Beebe, Kevan Berry, Leanne Bertani, Lydia Clement, Cathy Fonda, Anita Helms, Karen Heron, Rosalie Leone, Sylvia Lymer, Judith A. Lyons, Kathy Mackintosh, James and Christine Meager, Maureen Milton, Elaine Mitchell, Vickie Petrucelli, Brian Rix, Vanessa W. Rydhelm, Joy C. Sims, Albert Snyder, Meredith Johnson-Snyder, Linda Stebbins, Julie Sturman, Lamont M. Yoder.

Photographers: Richard G. Beauchamp, Zachary J. Brown, Cabal Photos, Lydia Clement, Farrar Photography, Isabell Francais, Anita Helms, Karen Heron, Sylvia Lymer, Meredith Johnson-Snyder, James Menzer, Elaine Mitchell, Jeannie Montford, Sharon and David Newcomb, O'Skot Photography, Robert Pearcy, Pet Portraits by Pam and Sherry, Alan Reznik, Russell Fine Art, Robert Smith, Pete Souza (The White House), Studio Eight, Julie Sturman, Chuck and Sandy Tatham, Betty Turner, Jerry Vavra Photography, Carol and Hank Williams, Barbara Wood.

The author acknowledges the contribution of Judy Iby for the following chapters: Sport of Purebred Dogs, Identification and Finding the Lost Dog, Traveling with Your Dog, Behavior and Canine Communication, and Health Care.

The portrayal of canine pet products in this book is for general instructive value only; the appearance of such products does not necessarily constitute an endorsement by the authors, the publisher, or the owners of the dogs portrayed in this book.

This book is dedicated to lovers of the Cavalier King Charles Spaniels everywhere and especially to Al and Lamont and our entire Rattlebridge family.

T.F.H. Publications, Inc.
One TFH Plaza
Third and Union Avenues
Neptune City, NJ 07753

www.tfhpublications.com

A NEW OWNER'S GUIDE TO
CAVALIER KING CHARLES SPANIELS

MEREDITH JOHNSON-SNYDER

Contents

2002 Edition

6 • History and Origin of the Cavalier King Charles Spaniel
Are Spaniels Spanish? • England Adopts the Toy Spaniels • The Cavalier in America

16 • Characteristics of the Cavalier
Think Carefully About Dog Ownership • The Case for the Purebred Dog • Life with a Cavalier • Male or Female? • The Cavalier Personality

30 • Selecting the Right Cavalier for You
Where to Buy Your Cavalier • Genetic Disorders • Recognizing a Healthy Puppy • Choosing a Show-Prospect Puppy • Puppy or Adult? • Identification Papers • Diet Sheet • Health Guarantee • Temperament and Socialization • The Adolescent Cavalier

A Cavalier's sweet and gentle expression is one feature that makes him so attractive.

52 • Standard of the Cavalier King Charles Spaniel

60 • Caring for Your Cavalier King Charles Spaniel
Feeding and Nutrition • Special Needs of the Cavalier

Raising two Cavalier puppies can be as easy as raising one.

70 • Grooming Your Cavalier King Charles Spaniel
Regular Coat Care • Bathing

78 • Housetraining and Training Your Cavalier
Thoughts on Training • Housetraining • Basic Training • Training Classes • Versatility

A healthy puppy will be bouncy, fun, extroverted, and playful.

100 • Sport
of Purebred Dogs
Puppy Kindergarten • Conformation •
Canine Good Citizen® • Obedience •
Tracking • Agility • Performance Tests •
General Information

116 • Health Care
The First Check Up • The Physical Exam
• Immunizations • Annual Visit •
Intestinal Parasites • Other Internal
Parasites • Heartworm Disease • External
Parasites • To Breed or Not To Breed

132 • Behavior and Canine
Communication
Canine Behavior • Socializing and
Training • Understanding the Dog's
Language • Body Language • Fear •
Aggression

144 • Dental Care
for Your Dog's Life

152 • Identification and
Finding the Lost Dog

154 • Traveling
with Your Dog
Trips • Air Travel • Boarding Kennel

Cavaliers love socializing with children and other Cavaliers.

159 • Resources

160 • Index

Who knows how far your Cavalier can go with the proper training?

HISTORY and Origin of the Cavalier King Charles Spaniel

Dogs of all breeds, from the smallest and most fragile to the largest, have one thing in common: All trace their history back through the ages to a common ancestor. As difficult as it may be to imagine when we look at the Cavalier King Charles Spaniel and compare it to a Great Dane or even a Bulldog, all three descend from what is known today as *Canis lupus*—-the wolf!

Exactly when the wolf came in from the forest and took up residence with its human counterparts is a matter of conjecture. However, most research determines that it was some time during the Mesolithic period, which was over 10,000 years ago. As these wolves became increasingly more domesticated, man undoubtedly realized he could direct their abilities to advantageously assist him in hunting and other survival pursuits.

Richard and Alice Feinnes, authors of *The Natural History of Dogs,* classify most dogs as having descended from one of four major groups, all of which are descendants of different branches of the wolf family. The classifications are the Dingo group, the Greyhound group, the Mastiff group, and the Northern or Arctic group.

Harana Howard of Sumara is an excellent example of a purebred Cavalier.

ARE SPANIELS SPANISH?

It is the Mastiff group that is of particular interest here. It is the branch of the family that evolved from mountain wolves such as the Tibetan wolf. The Mastiff group passed on certain special characteristics that have been inherited by many of the hunting breeds of today, including the pointers, the retrievers, and the spaniels.

It is important to note here that although many historians contribute the

This Blenheim Cavalier King Charles Spaniel is Eng. Ch. Lymrey Royal Reflection of Ricksbury, the top winning Cavalier of all time in England.

origin of the word "spaniel" to Spain itself, there are a good number of others who have researched the evolution of the dog and claim otherwise.

In *The Heritage of the Dog,* Colonel David Hancock traces the word "spaniel" to the ancient French verb *espanir,* which means to crouch or flatten. And looking back even further he finds that *espanir* is simply another corruption of the Old Latin *explanare,* meaning to flatten out.

Even as early as the days of ancient Rome, small spaniel-type dogs were used to drive game birds into nets. The dogs would then flatten themselves to the ground and falcons were sent in to dispatch the birds. Spaniel work was as important to the Roman hunter as it is to the hunter of today. Hancock also makes reference to an Old Italian verb *spaniare,* which means to escape from a net or trap. He also documents the fact that these early sporting spaniels were much smaller than are their modern-day descendants used in the field.

The Roman Empire's trade routes had immense cross-cultural effects. The routes reached as far as China and there we find a preponderance of small, short-nosed breeds.

There is frequent documentation of controlled breeding practices by the Romans occurring as early as the first century AD. The Romans categorized the many types of dogs into six general classifications. These categories are strikingly similar to the "variety groups" used as a classification method by the American Kennel Club today. Two thousand years ago, Romans wrote of "house guardian dogs, shepherd dogs, sporting dogs, war dogs, scent dogs, and sight dogs."

There can be little doubt that the small, short-nosed dogs of China were used effectively to reduce the size of the existing Roman sporting dogs. These smaller dogs became the ancestors of many breeds including the Maltese, Papillon, and the toy spaniels.

Because these dogs were small and attractive they ceased to live solely under the jurisdiction of the male population. The dogs were moving into homes throughout Europe as members of the family and becoming the property of women as well. Aristotle himself referred to these little dogs as the "ladies' favourite."

ENGLAND ADOPTS THE TOY SPANIELS

The small dogs traveled far and wide with their owners along the Roman trade routes and became highly prized gifts and items of barter.

Originally a sporting dog, the Cavalier became a favorite of the gentry of the day.

Jaron Chief's Ransom, owned by Karen Heron, is a lovely example of the rich red color of the Ruby Cavalier.

Toy spaniels of different origins can be seen in tapestries and paintings as early at the 15th, 16th, and 17th centuries in several European countries as well as in England.

These toy spaniels resembled smaller versions of the Cavaliers of today, with flattish skulls, feathery coats, and faces of varying degrees of length. They became favorites of the British royal courts, especially King Charles II, for whom the breed is named. It is also said that Mary Queen of Scots had a Cavalier.

According to Sheila Smith's *Cavalier King Charles Spaniels Today*, the Duke of Marlborough and his family formed a great liking for the little spaniels. In fact, for a period of time the breed came to be known as the Marlborough Spaniels. It was through the Duke's involvement in the Battle of Blenheim and the family's residence at Blenheim castle that the Marlborough Spaniels also became known both as the Blenheim and Marlborough red and white spaniels.

It was not too long afterward that the Cavalier as we know it today became nearly extinct when the flat-faced, domed-headed type came into vogue. Not everyone approved of this trend. Writing in his 1888 work, *The Dogs of Great Britain, America and Other Countries,* England's famed dog writer, Stonehenge, found the popular type to be, "… small delicate dogs, and though they have pretty good noses, and will hunt game readily, yet they so soon tire that they are rarely used for the purpose but are solely kept for their ornamental properties."

Stonehenge was not alone in his apparent deprecation of the fashion trend the little spaniel had taken. Hugh Dalziel was a knowledgeable and important figure in Great Britain's canine circles at the turn of the century. In his book, *British Dogs*, he states, "The modern Blenheim Spaniel is a very different dog from the original of that name so long kept by, and associated with, the Marlborough family. It is an instance of the breeder's skill exercised in a wrong direction, for the noseless specimens, with abnormally-developed skulls, I look upon as the results of a perverted taste, obtained at the sacrifice of intrinsic qualities, and without sufficient redeeming points to equalize the loss."

The ancestry of the Blenheim or Marlborough Spaniel can be traced to the Duke of Marlborough and his involvement in the Battle of Blenheim at Blenheim Castle.

It was not until 1926 that interest in the old-type Cavalier was revived. An American gentleman by the name of Roswell Eldridge, visiting England, was disappointed not to see the old-fashioned toy spaniels depicted in the paintings of the old masters and other works of art.

Eldridge offered a 25 pounds sterling prize at Crufts to run for five consecutive years and to be awarded to the best dog and bitch of the old-fashioned type spaniel. In 1928, a dog named Ann's

Former President Ronald Reagan and his prized Cavalier King Charles Spaniel. Photo by Pete Souza, The White House.

Fanciers and devotees of the original-type Cavalier revived the old character of the breed in 1926.

Son won the prize money and became the standard by which the breed was to be judged.

In that same year, a group of fanciers officially named the breed the Cavalier King Charles Spaniel and formed the Cavalier King Charles Club at the Crufts show. Their goal was to bring the old-fashioned toy spaniel back to life. A standard of excellence was drafted for the breed. In order to ensure themselves that the breed remained a natural one and would not drift off with fad and fashion, a clause was included in the standard that forbade trimming of any kind.

The devotees of the other flat-faced, high-domed variety continued on their way. Their dogs became known as the exotic and attractive King Charles Spaniel, or as they are known in America, the English Toy Spaniel.

In spite of continuing criticism from all quarters, the members of the Cavalier King Charles Club gave it their best toward the recognition of their dogs. Finally, in 1946 the Kennel Club of Great

Britain granted the Cavalier its first Challenge Certificates. The first club championship show was held in that same year.

Interest in the breed soared, attracting many of Great Britain's most knowledgeable dog men and women. Today, the Cavalier has one of the largest registrations of any breed in that country with entries in the hundreds at the major championship shows.

In 1973, John Evans took his young non-champion Alansmere Aquarius to the Crufts Dog Show. There, Aquarius won his second Challenge Certificate and was Best of Breed. The youngster did not stop there—he not only won the Toy Group but went on to win the supreme award—Best In Show, all breeds, under the highly respected Mr. Owen Gridley.

THE CAVALIER IN AMERICA

There are no records available of Cavaliers in the United States prior to the 1950s, but the breed does appear in American art often enough to lead one to believe the breed was even then more popular than it was "official." In 1952, however, Mrs. W. L. Lyons Brown of Kentucky brought a black and tan female Cavalier puppy back with her from England. As is the case in so many instances, Mrs. Brown found she could not stop "with just one." She not only became a breeder but also organized the Cavalier King Charles Spaniel Club, USA.

The organization's first show was held in 1962 with a respectable entry in the area of 35 Cavaliers. In the following years, the AKC gave the breed Miscellaneous Class recognition but there was no desire on the part of the Cavalier club to progress on to full AKC championship status.

The Canadian Kennel Club had given the breed full recognition in 1957, and there were those in the United States who felt the Cavalier should take

Ch. Lymrey Royal Scandal of Ricksbury shows the typical Cavalier expression.

The AKC first recognized the Cavalier King Charles Spaniel in 1994. Two years later, the breed became eligible for championship points as a member of the Toy Group.

The Cavalier comes in four acceptable colors: blenheim, tricolor, black and tan, and ruby.

its place along side the other respected AKC breeds as the breed did in their respective kennel clubs throughout the world.

When the AKC made it clearly evident that it planned to recognize the breed despite the reluctance of the parent club, a small group of devoted Cavalier breeders and exhibitors founded the American Cavalier King Charles Spaniel Club in 1994. The AKC recognized the new club as the official parent club in that same year.

On January 1, 1996, Cavalier King Charles Spaniels became eligible to compete for championship points as a member of the Toy Group. On the first weekend of competition, Wye Rebound of Rattlebridge, bred by Sally Bell and owned by Meredith Johnson-Snyder and Lamont Yoder, became the first American champion.

Predicting exciting things to come for the breed, there were two all-breed Bests In Show awarded to Cavaliers on that same first weekend. The first was Ch. Ravenrush Gillespie, bred and owned by John Gammon and Robert Schroll. The other was Ch. Luxxar Deep Ellum, bred and owned by Paula Campanozzi.

CHARACTERISTICS of the Cavalier

THINK CAREFULLY ABOUT DOG OWNERSHIP

Before anyone tries to decide whether or not a Cavalier is the correct breed for him or her, a larger and more important question must be asked. That question is, "Should I own a dog at all?" Dog ownership is a serious and time-consuming responsibility that should not be entered into lightly. Failure to understand this can make what should be a rewarding relationship one of sheer drudgery.

Not considering this in advance is one of the primary reasons for thousands upon thousands of unwanted dogs ending their lives in humane societies and animal shelters throughout America. Responsible Cavalier breeders dread the possibility of the breed becoming too popular for these very reasons.

If the prospective dog owner lives alone and conditions are conducive to dog ownership, all he or she needs to do is be sure that there is a strong desire to make the necessary commitment dog ownership entails. In the case of family households the situation is a much more complicated one. It is vital that the person who will actually be responsible for the dog's care really wants a dog.

In many households mothers are most often given the additional responsibility of caring for the family pets. Father is

Cavaliers can be hard to resist because of their sweet temperaments and loving nature.

While puppies are cute and lots of fun, they are also a big responsibility. Make sure the decision to add a Cavalier to your life is a carefully considered one.

away at the office all day. Children are busy with a myriad of school activities. Often it is the mother who is saddled with the additional chores of housebreaking, feeding, and trips to the veterinary hospital with what was supposed to be a family project. This situation often exists even when the mother of the family works out of the home.

Nearly all children love puppies and dogs and will promise anything to get one. But childhood enthusiasm can wane very quickly and it will be up to the adults in the family to ensure the dog receives proper care. Children should be taught responsibility, but to expect a living, breathing, and needy animal to teach a child this lesson is incredibly indifferent to the needs of the animal.

There are many households in which the entire family is gone from early morning until late in the day. The question that must then be asked is: Who will provide food for the dog and access to the outdoors if the dog is expected not to relieve itself in the house? This is something that can probably be worked out with an adult dog, but it is totally unfair for anyone to expect a young puppy to be left alone for the entire day.

Should an individual or family find they are capable of providing the proper home for a dog or young puppy, suitability of breed must

Adding a dog to your family will teach your child responsibility and respect for animals.

also be considered. Here it might be worthwhile to look at the difference between owning a purebred dog and one of mixed ancestry.

THE CASE FOR THE PUREBRED DOG

It goes without saying that a mixed-breed dog can give you as much love and devotion as a purebred dog. However, the manner in which the dog does this and how his personality, energy level, and the amount of care he requires suits an individual's lifestyle are major considerations. In a purebred dog, most of these considerations are predictable to a marked degree, even if the dog is purchased as a very young puppy. A puppy of uncertain parentage will not give you this assurance.

Most any puppy is cute and fairly manageable, but someone who lives in a small apartment will find life difficult with a dog that rapidly grows to the size of a Great Dane. Nor will the mountain climber or cross-country jogger be happy with a short-nosed breed that has difficulty catching his breath after simply walking across the street on a hot and humid summer day.

An owner who expects his or her dog to sit quietly by their side while they read or watch television is not going to be particularly happy with a high-strung, off-the-wall breed that finds sitting still for more than a few minutes difficult. The outdoorsman is certainly not going to be

No surprises here! When you bring home a purebred dog, you can expect he will have certain characteristics inherent to the breed.

happy with a dog whose voluminous coat attracts every burr and weed along the way.

Knowing what kind of dog best suits your lifestyle is not merely a consideration, it is paramount to the foundation of your lifelong relationship with the dog. If the dog you are considering does not fit your lifestyle, the relationship simply will not last.

LIFE WITH A CAVALIER

All of the foregoing applies to whether the Cavalier is your cup of tea or not. As appealing as the tiny Cavalier puppy might be, remember that he is a moderately long-haired dog that needs care to keep him happy and healthy. Regular brushing and frequent bathing is a must. When the Cavalier is outdoors it is no less a dog than most of its hunting dog relatives. The Cavalier will, without warning, bolt through the brush and take a cooling swim in the lake or roll in the mud like any other dog.

The Cavalier will continue to look like a Cavalier as long as you are willing to invest the time in keeping him that way. If you feel you do not have the time to attend to bathing and brushing, it will be necessary to have a professional groomer do this for you. If you appreciate the look of the breed, realize it will take more than a little effort on your part to keep your dog looking that way.

Dogs need attention, and the prospective owner must be sure that they can offer the time that is required of dog ownership.

The correct Cavalier coat is of moderate length and very silky. The coat is usually straight but occasionally there are dogs that possess a coat that has a slight wave. The Cavalier will shed like other dogs but regular brushing will keep the shedding to a minimum.

If you are willing to make the necessary commitment that a Cavalier requires, rest assured there are few breeds more versatile, amiable, and adaptable. While the Cavalier historically may well have been the pampered

Like all breeds of dogs, the Cavalier is susceptible to genetic diseases. It is important that you seek responsible breeders. Sylvia Lymer poses with two lovely young girls.

Children love the friendly Cavalier and this versatile and flexible breed can fit into most loving and caring household environments.

pet of European dignitaries and has spent his nights tucked under the covers of many a royal bed, never forget the Cavalier's gun-dog heritage.

If responsibly bred, the Cavalier is a hardy breed and seldom prone to chronic illnesses with the exception of mitral valve disease discussed later. For its size, the breed has amazing energy, great strength, and hardly knows the meaning of fear. The breed is large enough for well-behaved children who are old enough to understand how to properly handle a dog. The man of the household can also take pride in owning him, the smallest of the hunting spaniels. The breed is small enough so that an owner needs not be an amateur weightlifter to easily handle a Cavalier.

The Cavalier is extremely playful and inquisitive. It is a breed that never ceases to find something interesting to do. Yet a Cavalier loves to sit by your side or on your lap when you read or listen to music. Introduced early enough and properly supervised, the Cavalier can coexist with a cat, rabbit, or even larger dog as well as he can with humans.

Don't forget the Cavalier's hunting heritage, however. Some can be taught to flush birds and retrieve. One of the Cavaliers we have bred has become a junior hunter.

Little creatures that scurry away will soon find the Cavalier hot on their heels. Therefore, the breed cannot be trusted off lead if there is any danger of traffic. Cavaliers also have no fear of other dogs, large or small. Larger, less amiable dogs may mistake the Cavalier's outgoing attitude as aggression and react accordingly. Three words to the wise—Cavaliers are "always on leash." A fenced yard is an absolute must for the owner of this breed!

Of this breed, it can be said without hesitation that two dogs are just as easy, or sometimes easier, to raise than one. The breed loves his own and when there are several together they can be found sleeping piled one on top of the other.

MALE OR FEMALE?

While the sex of a dog in many breeds is a very important consideration, this is not particularly the case with the Cavalier. The male Cavalier makes just as loving, devoted, and trainable a companion as the female. In fact, there are some who believe a male Cavalier can be even more devoted to his master.

Double your fun! Many feel that raising two Cavalier puppies is just as easy, if not easier, than raising one.

There is one important point to consider in determining your choice between male and female. While both must be trained not to relieve themselves just anywhere in the home, males have a natural instinct to lift their leg and urinate to "mark" their home territory. It seems confusing to many dog owners, but a male's marking of his home turf has absolutely nothing to do with whether or not he is housebroken. The two responses come from entirely different needs and each must be dealt with in that manner. Some dogs are more difficult than others to train against marking within the confines of the household. Males that are used for breeding are even more prone to this response and are harder to break of this habit.

On the other hand, females have their semiannual "heat" cycles once they have reached sexual maturity. In the case of the female Cavalier, this can occur for the first time from six to ten months of age. These cycles are accompanied by a vaginal discharge that creates the need to confine the female for about three weeks so that she does not soil her surroundings. It must be understood the female has no control over this bloody discharge, so it has nothing to do with training.

Cavaliers love their own. When they are together, they can usually be found sleeping one on top of the other.

Spaying or neutering your Cavalier will help prevent certain diseases and control the pet population.

While most Cavaliers are not normally left outdoors by themselves for long stretches of time, this is one time a female should not be out by herself for even a brief movement or two. The need for confinement and keeping a careful watch over the female in heat is especially important to prevent her becoming pregnant by some neighborhood Lothario. Equally dangerous to her well-being is the male that is much larger than your Cavalier female. The male may be too large to actually breed her but he could seriously injure or even kill her in his attempts to do so.

For both the male and female, sexually related problems can be entirely eliminated by spaying the female and neutering of the male. Unless a Cavalier has been purchased expressly for breeding or showing from a breeder capable of making this judgment, your dog should be sexually altered.

Breeding and raising puppies should be left in the hands of people who have the facilities to keep each and every puppy they breed until the correct home is found for it. This can often take many months after a litter is born. Most single dog owners are not equipped to this. Naturally, a responsible Cavalier owner would never allow his or her pet to roam the streets and end his life in an animal shelter. Unfortunately, being forced to place a puppy due to space constraints before you are able to thoroughly check out the prospective buyer may in fact create this exact situation.

Many times we have had parents ask to buy a female "just as a pet," but with the intention of breeding her so that their children can witness the birth process. There are countless books and videos now available that portray this wonderful event and do not add to the worldwide pet overpopulation we now face. Altering one's companion dogs not only precludes the possibility of adding to this problem, it eliminates bothersome household problems and precautions.

It should be understood, however, that spaying and neutering are not reversible procedures. Spayed females or neutered males are not allowed to be shown in American Kennel Club conformation shows, nor will altered animals ever be able to be used for breeding. Altered animals can be shown in obedience and many other areas of competition.

THE CAVALIER PERSONALITY

Historically, the Cavalier has been a close companion to man. Whether the darling of the royal courts or trudging beside his owner on a day in the field, everything the little spaniels have done, they have done in the company of humans. It is only truly happy when allowed to continue that association. It simply would not do for a Cavalier to be shut away in a kennel or outdoor run with only occasional access to your life and environment. Should this be your intent, another breed would best serve you. The very essence of the Cavalier is in his unique personality and sensitive, loving nature that is best developed by constant human contact.

This should not be construed to mean that only people who are home all day to cater to every whim of their dog can be a Cavalier owner. We know many working people who are away most of the day whose Cavaliers are well mannered and trustworthy when left home alone. The key here seems to be the quality rather than the quantity of time spent with their pet. Morning or evening walks, grooming sessions, game time, and simply having your Cavalier

Ch. Grantilly Secret Love of Ambleside owned by Julie Sturman.

share your life when you are home is vital to the breed's personality development and attitude. A Cavalier likes to be talked to and praised.

Cavaliers are "attachment dogs." They are extremely affectionate and can't get close enough to their people. Even five-week-old puppies will instinctively press their little cheeks against a person's face. They simply want to be close. They are very trusting and totally devoted. The Cavalier is seldom a one-man dog, preferring to spread their affection to everyone they come in contact with.

The Cavalier clings—not out of insecurity but out of their unquenchable thirst for closeness. Sleeping with a Cavalier can present problems though, particularly with small children as the breed will often attempt to sleep on their loved one's head or face, which can inhibit breathing.

At the same time, however, the breed can be very independent if they are focusing on a bird or other wildlife. Do not expect your Cavalier—even the best-trained dog—to abandon the chase once it has taken after a bird or rabbit.

Within the confines of his own household, a Cavalier can prove to be an excellent watchdog in the sense that he will sound the alarm if he sees or hears anything unusual. Expect your Cavalier to let you know the doorbell has rung or that someone is knocking at the door. On the other hand, you will not be disturbed by constant and needless barking.

The Cavalier loves to please his owner and is highly trainable, as long as the trainer is not heavy-handed. Training problems encountered are far more apt to be due to the owner, rather than due to the dog not understanding what is to be learned.

Too many Cavalier owners are inclined to think of their companions as "little people." It must be understood that the Cavalier is

Cavaliers have an unquenchable thirst to be close to someone they love.

No matter how cute a puppy is, one must not mistake him for a little person.

first and foremost a *dog.* Dogs, like the wolves from which they descend, are pack animals and need a pack leader. Dogs are now totally dependent upon humans to provide that leadership. When leadership is not provided, a dog can easily become confused and neurotic.

Setting boundaries is important to the well-being of any dog and the Cavalier is no exception. The sooner your dog understands there are rules that must be obeyed, the easier it will be for it to become an enjoyable companion.

The amount of time in which you learn to establish and enforce those rules will determine how quickly this will come about. The Cavalier is not vindictive or particularly stubborn but he does need guidance in order to achieve his potential.

SELECTING the Right Cavalier for You

WHERE TO BUY YOUR CAVALIER

The Cavalier you buy will live with you for many years to come. It is not the least bit unusual for an intelligently bred, healthy Cavalier to live as long as 10 or 12 years of age. Obviously, it is important that the Cavalier you select has the advantage of beginning life in a healthy environment and that he comes from sound, healthy stock.

The only way you can be sure of this is to go directly to a breeder who has earned a reputation over the years for consistently producing Cavaliers that are mentally and physically sound. A breeder is able to earn this reputation through a well-planned breeding program that has been governed by rigid selectivity. Selective breeding programs are aimed at maintaining the many fine qualities of the Cavalier and eliminating any genetic weaknesses.

So many choices and so many happy Cavaliers! Pick the dog that will fit into your family and lifestyle.

Not every puppy will grow up to be a show-quality dog, but that will not stop him from being an excellent and loving companion.

Breeders who successfully show Cavaliers usually breed for themselves. In every litter, they hope for show puppies and give each and every puppy the care that will bring him to his full potential. But certainly not every puppy will make the grade for the show ring and these will be available as companions.

This process is both time consuming and costly for a breeder, but it ensures the buyer of getting a dog that will be a joy to own. Responsible Cavalier breeders protect their investment by basing their breeding programs on the healthiest, most representative stock available and providing each succeeding generation with the very best care and nutrition.

It can be extremely risky to buy a Cavalier through a newspaper advertisement or from any source unaware of the genetic background of their puppies. The seller should also be personally familiar with the kind of care that was given to the puppy from birth until the time you see him. Many individuals are now breeding for profit alone and care less about the problems you may encounter with the puppy they sell you.

Genetic Disorders

Cavaliers can suffer from many of the same health problems as other breeds, like genetic eye disorders such as cataracts and retinal dysplasia. Like many breeds, the Cavalier can be subject to slipping patellas and hip dysplasia. Problems such as these do not usually inhibit a Cavalier from leading a normal life.

It is important to be aware, however, that there is a very high incidence of mitral valve heart disease in the Cavalier King Charles Spaniel. By age ten it is very common for most Cavaliers to have developed a heart murmur. The onset of a murmur at a young age can signify mitral valve disease, which can lead to premature death if it is severe enough. No one can predict mitral valve disease. It crops up in every bloodline and can occur even if the parents are clear. Reputable breeders will have their dogs checked by a cardiologist annually and will only breed dogs with clear hearts. You should be able to obtain a statement signifying this from the breeder.

Sometimes a puppy will exhibit a puppy murmur that goes away in a few months and is nothing to worry about. A puppy that evidences a heart problem should be watched carefully and checked for mitral valve disease by special testing done by a cardiologist.

The governing kennel clubs and the Cavalier King Charles Spaniel breed clubs of the world maintain lists of breeders that can assist a prospective Cavalier buyer in locating responsible breeders

Good breeding practices will help protect your Cavalier from genetic diseases.

Make sure to contact the AKC, the American Cavalier King Charles Spaniel Club, or a local kennel club when trying to find a responsible Cavalier breeder.

of quality stock. If you are not sure of where to find an established breeder in your area, we strongly recommend contacting your local kennel club, the American Cavalier King Charles Spaniel Club, Inc., or the AKC for recommendations.

It is likely that you will be able to find an established Cavalier breeder in your own area. If so, you will be able to visit the breeder, inspect the premises, and in many cases, also be able to see a puppy's parents and other relatives. These breeders are always willing and able to discuss any problems that might exist in the breed and how they should be dealt with.

Should there be no breeders in your immediate area you can arrange to have a puppy shipped to you. There are good breeders throughout the country who have shipped puppies to satisfied owners out of state and even to other countries. Be careful—never hesitate to ask the breeder you visit or deal with any questions or concerns you might have relative to owning a Cavalier.

You should expect the breeder to ask you a good number of questions as well. Good breeders are just as interested in placing their puppies in a loving and safe environment as you are in obtaining a happy, healthy puppy.

It is extremely important that your Cavalier puppy comes from a breeder who is dedicated to producing animals that are sound of both mind and body.

Not all quality breeders maintain large kennels. In fact, you are more apt to find that Cavaliers that come from the homes of small hobby breeders who keep just a few dogs and only have occasional litters. The names of these people are as likely to appear on the recommended lists from kennel clubs as the larger kennels that maintain many dogs. Hobby breeders are equally dedicated to breeding quality Cavaliers and have the distinct advantage of being able to raise their puppies in a home environment with all the accompanying personal attention and socialization.

Again, it is important that both the buyer and the seller ask questions. We would be highly suspicious of a person who is willing to sell you a Cavalier puppy with no questions asked.

RECOGNIZING A HEALTHY PUPPY

Most Cavalier breeders are apt to keep their puppies until they are 10 to 14 weeks of age and have been given all of their puppy inoculations. By the time the litter is eight weeks old it is normally entirely weaned, no longer nursing on their mother. While the puppies were nursing they had complete immunity from disease from their mother. Once they have stopped nursing, however, they become highly susceptible to many infectious diseases. A number of these diseases can be transmitted on the hands and clothing of humans. Therefore it is extremely important that your puppy is current on all the shots he must have for his age.

Selecting a Puppy

A healthy Cavalier puppy is normally a bouncy, playful extrovert. We have found that Cavalier puppies mature a bit slower and at different individual rates than many other breeds. They also seem to go through normal puppy fear periods at different times than

You can easily find a great Cavalier puppy from a small hobby breeder. Make sure the puppies look healthy, clean, and well taken care of.

Take precautions and make sure your puppy is up to date on all shots required for his age before taking him out to make friends.

other breeds. A quiet and reserved puppy of four weeks may be a holy terror a few weeks later.

When we had our first Cavalier litter we were worried sick that the puppies were retarded, as they did not seem to progress as quickly as other breeds we knew. We had to learn by experience that Cavalier puppies remain "lumps" longer than other breeds and display very little ambition to grow up.

If at all possible, take the available puppy into a different room of the kennel or house. The smells will remain the same for the puppy so he should still feel secure, but this will give you an opportunity to see how the puppy acts away from his littermates and it will also give you time to inspect the puppy more closely.

Even though Cavalier puppies are very small, they should feel sturdy to the touch. They should not feel bony, nor should their abdomens be bloated or extended. A puppy that has just eaten may have a full belly, but the puppy should never appear obese.

A healthy puppy's ears will be pink and clean. Dark discharge or a bad odor could indicate ear mites, a sure sign of lack of cleanliness and poor maintenance. A Cavalier puppy's breath should always smell sweet. His teeth must be clean and bright and there should never be any malformation of the jaw, lips, or nostrils.

A Cavalier puppy's eyes are dark and clear. Runny eyes, or eyes that appear red and irritated, could be caused by a myriad of problems. Their eyes will often tear when teething.

Coughing or diarrhea are danger signals, as is any discharge from the nose or eruptions on the skin. The skin should be clean and the coat soft, clean, and lustrous.

Sound conformation can be determined even at eight or ten weeks of age. The puppy's legs should be straight without bumps or malformations. The little toes should point straight ahead.

The puppy's attitude tells you a great deal about his state of health. Puppies that are feeling "out of sorts" will usually find a warm littermate to snuggle up to and prefer to stay that way even when the rest of the "gang" wants to play or go exploring.

Again, a good breeder knows what you need to be concerned about and what may simply be a developmental stage. A breeder of quality Cavaliers can be relied upon. Someone who does nothing but raise puppies for resale is a dangerous risk.

CHOOSING A SHOW-PROSPECT PUPPY

If you or your family are considering a show career for your puppy we strongly advise putting yourself in the hands of an established breeder who has earned a reputation for breeding winning show dogs. They alone are most capable of anticipating what one might expect a young puppy from their line to develop into when he reaches maturity.

A healthy puppy will be a bouncy, fun, extroverted, and playful dog that is curious about the world around him.

A knowledgeable breeder will help you pick the best show prospect from a litter of Cavaliers.

Although the potential buyer should read the American Kennel Club standard of perfection for the Cavalier, it is hard for the novice to really understand the nuances of what is being asked for. The experienced breeder is best equipped to do so and will be only too happy to assist you in your quest. Even at that, no one can make accurate predictions or guarantees on a very young puppy.

Any predictions a

Keep your Cavalier puppy occupied and out of trouble. Make sure he has plenty of toys and a safe place in which to play.

breeder is apt to make are based upon the breeder's experience with past litters that produced winning showdogs. It should be obvious that the more successful a breeder has been in producing winning Cavaliers through the years, the broader his or her basis of comparison will be.

The most any responsible breeder will say about a 12-week-old puppy is that it has "show potential." If you are serious about showing your Cavalier, we, like most other breeders, strongly suggest waiting until a puppy is from 6 to 12 months old before making any decisions. It only makes sense to assume that the older the puppy, the easier it will be to determine how he will turn out.

The Cavalier standard prefers "a perfect, regular and complete scissors bite, i.e., the upper teeth closely overlapping the lower teeth and set square in the jaws." However, permanent teeth come in at six months old and until that time, bites (how the teeth are aligned) are completely uncertain in this breed. In fact, as many breeders will tell you, bites can continue to change until the Cavalier is as old as 24 months. Do not forget the flat-faced, high-domed dogs that hover in the Cavalier's genetic makeup. This heritage makes predictability of mouth development difficult, if not impossible.

What looks like proper size for a show Cavalier at three months of age can change drastically by the time the puppy matures. Coat texture can often change significantly as well.

There are many other "beauty point" shortcomings a Cavalier puppy might have that would in no way interfere with him being a wonderful companion, but these faults would be serious drawbacks in the show ring. Many of these flaws are such that a beginner in the breed would hardly notice. Things such as extremely heavy markings, one or no testicles for a male, an incorrect topline, or tail carried vertically would not keep your Cavalier from being a happy, healthy, and loving companion. These faults, however, would keep it from ever becoming a winner.

This is why employing the assistance of a good breeder is so important. Still, the prospective buyer should be at least generally aware of what the Cavalier show puppy should look like.

All of the aforementioned points regarding soundness and health of the pet puppy apply to the show puppy as well. The show prospect must not only be sound and healthy, it must adhere to the standard of the breed very closely.

The complete standard of the breed appears in this book and there are also a number of other books that can assist the newcomer

When he was a pup, Can. Ch. Dreamwoods Phoenix Rising's nearly perfect black and tan markings made him an easy bet for life as a show dog.

Even if a career as a show dog is not in your Cavalier's future, he will still make a loving pet.

to learn more about the Cavalier. The more you know about the history and origin of the breed, the better equipped you will be to see the differences that distinguish the show dog from the pet.

Puppy or Adult?

For the person anticipating a show career for their Cavalier or for someone hoping to become a breeder, the purchase of a young adult provides greater certainty with respect to quality. Even those who simply want a companion can consider the adult dog.

From a breeder's point of view, Cavaliers act like puppies their entire lives and readily adapt to new places and people quite easily. In some instances, breeders will have males or females they no longer wish to use for breeding and after the dogs have been altered would prefer to have them live out their lives in a private home with all its attendant care and attention. In the private home environment the dog will become the "one and only" instead of one of many.

Acquiring an adult dog eliminates the many problems raising a puppy involves, and Cavaliers, unlike some other breeds, do transfer to new homes well. They love to be with humans and though many of us hate to admit it, most Cavaliers will be just as content living with one person as they are with another, just so long as they are loved and well cared for.

Elderly people often prefer the adult dog, particularly one that is housebroken because they are easier to manage and require less supervision and damage control. Adult Cavaliers are seldom chewers and are usually more than ready to adapt to household rules.

There are things to consider though. Adult dogs have usually developed behaviors that may or may not fit into your routine. If a Cavalier has never been exposed to small children the dog may be totally perplexed, often frightened, by this new experience. Children are also inclined to be more active and vocal than the average adult is and this could intimidate the dog as well.

We strongly advise taking an adult dog on a trial basis to see if the dog will adapt to the new owner's lifestyle and environment. Most often it works, but on rare occasions a prospective owner decides that training his or her dog from puppyhood is worth the time and effort it requires.

IDENTIFICATION PAPERS

The purchase of any purebred dog entitles you to three very important documents: a health record that includes an inoculation or "shot" record, a copy of the dog's pedigree, and the registration certificate.

Inoculations

You will find that most Cavalier breeders have initiated the necessary preliminary inoculation series for their puppies by the

Although a Cavalier is blessed with a divinely innocent look, do not underestimate a puppy's ability to find his way into mischief.

At the ripe old age of three months, Park Place Fair Weather at Ambleside has aspirations for the big time.

time they are 12 weeks of age. These inoculations temporarily protect the puppies against hepatitis, leptospirosis, distemper, and canine parvovirus. "Permanent" inoculations will follow at a prescribed time. Since different breeders and veterinarians follow different approaches to inoculations, it is extremely important that the health record you obtain for your puppy accurately lists what shots have been given and when. In this way the veterinarian you choose will be able to continue with the appropriate inoculation series as needed. In most cases, rabies inoculations are not given until a puppy is six months of age or older.

Pedigree

The pedigree is your dog's "family tree." The breeder must supply you with a copy of this document authenticating your puppy's ancestors back to at least the third generation. All purebred dogs have pedigrees. The pedigree in itself does not mean that your puppy is of show quality. All it means is that all of its ancestors were in fact registered Cavalier King Charles Spaniels. They may all have been of pet quality. Unscrupulous puppy dealers often try to imply that a pedigree indicates that all dogs having one are of championship caliber. This is not true. Again, it simply tells you all of the dog's ancestors are purebred.

Carefully supervised Cavaliers raised with children establish a bond that is a rare and wonderful thing to behold.

A pleasantly plump Cavalier litter at just a few days of age. Cavalier puppies will need to be vaccinated while young to protect against certain diseases.

Registration Certificate

The registration certificate is the canine world's "birth certificate." A country's governing kennel club issues this certificate. When you transfer the ownership of your Cavalier from the breeder's name to your own name, the transaction is entered on this certificate and, once mailed to the appropriate kennel club, it is permanently recorded in their computerized files. You will then be sent a copy of the amended certificate.

Keep all of your dog's documents in a safe place as you will need them when you visit your veterinarian or should you ever wish to breed or show your Cavalier. Keep the name, address, and phone number of the breeder from whom you purchase your Cavalier in a separate place as well. Should you ever lose any of these important documents, you will then be able to contact the breeder so that you may obtain duplicates.

DIET SHEET

Your Cavalier is the happy, healthy puppy he is because the breeder has been carefully feeding and caring for him. Every breeder we know has his or her own particular way of doing this. Most breeders give the new owner a written record that details the amount and kind of food

Aside from size and amount of hair, the Cavalier puppy clearly and distinctly resembles what he will look like when mature.

a puppy has been receiving. Follow these recommendations to the letter at least for the first month or two after the puppy comes to live with you.

The diet sheet should indicate the number of times a day your Cavalier has been accustomed to being fed and the kind of vitamin supplementation, if any, he has been receiving. Following the prescribed procedure will reduce the chance of upset stomach and loose stools.

Usually, a breeder's diet sheet projects the increases and changes in food that will be necessary as your puppy grows from week to week. If the sheet does not include this information, ask the breeder for suggestions regarding increases and the eventual changeover to adult food.

In the unlikely event you are not supplied with a diet sheet by the breeder and are unable to get one, your veterinarian will be able to advise you in this respect. There are countless foods now being manufactured expressly to meet the nutritional needs of puppies and growing dogs. A trip down the pet aisle at your supermarket will prove just how many choices you have. Two important tips to remember: read labels carefully for content, and when dealing with established, reliable manufacturers, you are more likely to get what you pay for. Feeding and nutrition are dealt with in detail in the chapter on caring for your Cavalier.

Make sure the breeder from whom you purchase your Cavalier supplies you with the dog's diet sheet in order to avoid stomach upsets.

Your Cavalier's pedigree indicates that all of his ancestors are purebred dogs.

HEALTH GUARANTEE

Any reputable breeder is more than willing to supply a written agreement that the purchase of your Cavalier is contingent upon his passing a veterinarian's examination. Ideally, you will be able to arrange for an appointment with your chosen veterinarian right after you have picked up your puppy from the breeder and before you take the puppy home. If this is not possible you should not delay this procedure any longer than 24 hours from the time you take your puppy home.

TEMPERAMENT AND SOCIALIZATION

Temperament is both hereditary and environmental. Poor treatment and lack of proper socialization can ruin inherited good temperament. A Cavalier puppy that comes from shy, nervous, or aggressive stock, or one that exhibits those characteristics himself, will make a poor companion or show dog and should certainly never be bred. Therefore, it is critical that you obtain a happy puppy from a breeder who is determined to produce good temperament, and has taken all the necessary steps early on to provide the early socialization necessary.

Temperaments in the same litter can range from confident and outgoing on the high end of the scale to shy and fearful at the low end, but by and large, Cavalier temperament is and should be delightful. As we have stated previously, this temperament is a hallmark of the breed.

If you are fortunate enough to have older children in the household who are old enough to understand a Cavalier puppy's needs, your socialization task will be assisted considerably. The two seem to understand each other and in some way known only to the puppies and children themselves, they give each other the confidence to face the trying ordeal of growing up.

Every visitor that enters your household should be introduced to your Cavalier. Usually, this is completely unnecessary as your puppy will take care of all those formalities on his own.

Your puppy should go everywhere with you: The post office, the market, the shopping mall—wherever. Be prepared to create a stir wherever you go because the very thing that attracted you to the first Cavalier you met will apply for other people as well. Everyone will want to pet your little companion and there is nothing in the world better for him.

Well-supervised and gentle children are wonderful playmates for Cavalier puppies.

Girl's best friend! Children and puppies seem to understand each other when it comes to the trials of growing up.

Should your puppy back off from a stranger, pick him up and hand him to the person. The young Cavalier will quickly learn that all humans—young and old, short and tall, and of all races—are friends. You are in charge. You must call the shots.

If your Cavalier has a show career in its future, there are other things in addition to just being handled that will have to be taught. All show dogs must learn to have their mouths inspected by the judge. The judge must also be able to check the teeth. Males must be accustomed to having their testicles touched, as the dog show judge must determine that all male dogs are "complete," which means there are two normal-sized testicles in the scrotum. These inspections must begin in puppyhood and be done on a regular and continuing basis.

The Adolescent Cavalier

At any time from about 10 or 11 months of age the Cavalier coat can begin to change. Your puppy, in addition to growing more independent, will stop developing his adult coat. When this happens, mats may appear where new hair growth meets already existing hair. While it does not always happen, some dogs are more prone to this matting than others. Thorough brushing will only take a few minutes so it should be done every day to check on the coat's condition and keep it mat free.

It is important that you attend to these grooming sessions regularly during the early months of your puppy's growth. If your Cavalier has been groomed regularly as a puppy, you will find your task is much easier when you are working with the more abundant adult coat. More detailed grooming instructions are given in the chapter dealing with bathing and grooming your Cavalier King Charles Spaniel.

Food needs to be changed during this growth period. Some Cavaliers seem as if they can never get enough to eat while others eat just enough to avoid starvation. Think of Cavalier puppies as individualistic as children and act accordingly.

Purebred dog experts agree that a Cavalier should be entirely recognizable, even if all that can be seen is the dog's head.

The amount of food you give your Cavalier should be adjusted to how much he will readily consume at each meal. If the entire meal is eaten quickly, add a small amount to the next feeding and continue to do so as the need increases. This method will ensure that you give your puppy enough food, but you must also pay close attention to the dog's appearance and condition, as you do not want a puppy to become overweight or obese.

The adolescent stage is an important one for Cavaliers because it is the time they must learn all the household rules by which they will be expected to live.

At eight weeks of age a Cavalier puppy is eating four meals a day. By the time he is six months old, the puppy can do well on two meals a day, with perhaps a snack in the middle of the day. If your puppy does not eat the food offered, he is either not hungry or not well. Your dog will eat when he is hungry. If you suspect that the dog is not well, a trip to the veterinarian is immediately in order.

This adolescent period is a particularly important one as it is the time your Cavalier must learn all the household and social rules by which he will live for the rest of his life. Your patience and commitment during this time will not only produce a respected canine good citizen but will forge a bond between the two of you that will grow and ripen into a wonderful relationship.

STANDARD of the Cavalier King Charles Spaniel

The Cavalier King Charles Spaniel is blessed with a royal heritage of breed type. The AKC standard is well written, closely parallels its precursor, the British standard, and demands that the Cavalier remain a naturally beautiful (no clipping or trimming for the show ring!) breed whose sterling temperament makes him a joy to behold. As a result, we have in America a toy breed of unparalleled beauty that could easily win a Toy Group yet maintains all the characteristics of soundness and movement that would stand against any sporting dog it might come up against.

Like any standard of perfection, the implications of the Cavalier standard take many years to fully understand. This can only be accomplished by observing many quality Cavaliers over the years and reading as much about the breed as possible. Many books have been written about the breed and reading them is well worth the owner's time and effort if he or she is interested in showing or breeding this breed.

It should be remembered that the breed standard describes the "perfect" Cavalier, but no dog is perfect and no Cavalier, not even the greatest dog show winner, will possess every quality asked for in its perfect form. It is how closely an individual dog adheres to the standard of the breed that determines its show potential.

These two Ruby beauties are owned by Lydia Clement.

The fact that the Cavalier is a toy breed does not mean he should be delicate or unsound. He should possess well-made limbs and a sturdy body.

Just because it is a toy breed, there is no reason for the Cavalier to be unsound. The standard's requirements for construction reveal well-made limbs and an easy way of moving. The breed's balanced construction permits graceful, easy movement. Since the breed standard describes very normal construction and does not call for any unusual features of construction, there should be no physical abnormalities.

STANDARD OF THE CAVALIER KING CHARLES SPANIEL

General Appearance

The Cavalier King Charles Spaniel is an active, graceful, well-balanced toy spaniel, very gay and free in action; fearless and sporting in character, yet at the same time gentle and affectionate. It is this typical gay temperament, combined with true elegance and royal appearance which are of paramount importance in the breed. Natural appearance with no trimming, sculpting or artificial alteration is essential to breed type.

The Cavalier's head must be in proportion to the rest of the body, not too large or too small in relation to the overall size of the dog.

Size, Proportion, Substance

Size—Height 12 to 13 inches at the withers; weight proportionate to height, between 13 and 18 pounds. A small, well balanced dog within these weights is desirable, but these are ideal heights and weights and slight variations are permissible. *Proportion*—The body approaches squareness, yet if measured from point of shoulder to point of buttock, is slightly longer than the height at the withers. The height from the withers to the elbow is approximately equal to the height from the elbow to the ground. *Substance*—Bone moderate in proportion to size. Weedy and coarse specimens are to be equally penalized.

Head

Proportionate to size of dog, appearing neither too large nor too small for the body. *Expression*—The sweet, gentle, melting expression is an important breed characteristic. *Eyes*—Large, round, but not prominent and set well apart; color a warm, very dark brown; giving a lustrous, limpid look. Rims dark. There should be cushioning under the eyes which contributes to the soft expression. *Faults*—small, almond-shaped, prominent, or light eyes; white surrounding ring. *Ears*—Set high, but not close, on top of the head. Leather long with plenty

Remember that no Cavalier can perfectly represent the standard, but a purebred dog should be as true to form as possible.

of feathering and wide enough so that when the dog is alert, the ears fan slightly forward to frame the face. *Skull*—Slightly rounded, but without dome or peak; it should appear flat because of the high placement of the ears. Stop is moderate, neither filled nor deep. *Muzzle*—Full muzzle slightly tapered. Length from base of stop to tip of nose about 1 1/2 inches. Face well filled below eyes. Any tendency towards snipiness undesirable. Nose pigment uniformly black without flesh marks and nostrils well developed. *Lips* well developed but not pendulous giving a clean finish. *Faults*—Sharp or pointed muzzles. *Bite*—A perfect, regular and complete scissors bite is preferred, i.e., the upper teeth closely overlapping the lower teeth and set square into the jaws. *Faults*—undershot bite, weak or crooked teeth, crooked jaws.

The Cavalier should possess large, dark, round eyes and a sweet expression.

Neck, Topline, Body

Neck—Fairly long, without throatiness, well enough muscled to form a slight arch at the crest. Set smoothly into nicely sloping shoulders to give an elegant look. *Topline*—Level both when moving and standing. *Body*—Short-coupled with ribs well spring but not barrelled. Chest moderately deep, extending to elbows allowing ample heart room. Slightly less body at the flank than at the last rib, but with no tucked-up appearance. *Tail*—Well set on, carried happily but never much above the level of the back, and in constant characteristic motion when the dog is in action. Docking is optional. If docked, no more than one third to be removed.

Forequarters

Shoulders well laid back. *Forelegs* straight and well under the dog with elbows close to the sides. *Pasterns* strong and feet compact with well-cushioned pads. Dewclaws may be removed.

Hindquarters

The hindquarters construction should come down from a good broad pelvis, moderately muscled; stifles well turned and hocks well let down. The hindlegs when viewed from the rear

What makes the Cavalier so well loved are features unique only to this breed.

The coat of the Cavalier should be of moderate length, silky, and free from curl. A slight wave is permissible.

should parallel each other from hock to heel. *Faults:* cow or sickle hocks.

Coat

Of moderate length, silky, free from curl. Slight wave permissible. Feathering on ears, chest, legs and tail should be long, and the feathering on the feet is a feature of the breed. No trimming of the dog is permitted. *Specimens where the coat has been altered by trimming, clipping, or by artificial means shall be so severly penalized as to be effectively eliminated from competition.* Hair growing between the pads on the underside of the feet may be trimmed.

Color

Blenheim—Rich chestnut markings well broken up on a clear, pearly white ground. The ears must be chestnut and the color evenly spaced on the head and surrounding both eyes,

Park Place Fair Weather at Ambleside has the representative tricolor markings of this color of Cavalier King Charles Spaniel.

with a white blaze between the eyes and ears, in the center of which may be the lozenge or "Blenheim spot". The lozenge is a unique and desirable, though not essential, characteristic of the Blenheim. *Tricolor*—Jet black markings well broken up on a clear, pearly white ground. The ears must be black and the color evenly spaced on the head and surrounding both eyes, with a white blaze between the eyes. Rich tan markings over the eyes, on cheeks, inside ears and on underside of tail. *Ruby*—Whole-colored rich red. *Black and Tan*—Jet black with rich, bright tan markings over eyes, on cheeks, inside ears, on chest, legs, and on underside of tail. *Faults*—Heavy ticking on Blenheims or Tricolors, white marks on Rubies or Black and Tans.

A Blenheim-colored coat must have rich chestnut markings that are well broken up on a clear, pearly white ground.

Gait

Free moving and elegant in action, with good reach in front and sound, driving rear action. When viewed from the side, the movement exhibits a good length of stride, and viewed from front and rear it is straight and true, resulting from straight-boned fronts and properly made and muscled hindquarters.

Temperament

Gay, friendly, non-aggressive with no tendency towards nervousness or shyness. *Bad temper, shyness, and meanness are not to be tolerated and are to be severely penalized as to effectively remove the specimen from competition.*

Approved Date: January 10, 1995.
Effective Date: April 30, 1995.

CARING for Your Cavalier King Charles Spaniel

FEEDING AND NUTRITION

The best way to make sure your Cavalier puppy is obtaining the right amount and the correct type of food for his age is to follow the diet or maintenance sheet provided by the breeder from whom you obtain your puppy. Do your best not to change the puppy's diet and you will be less apt to run into digestive problems and diarrhea. Diarrhea is very serious in young puppies. Puppies with diarrhea can dehydrate very rapidly, causing severe problems and even death.

If it is necessary to change your Cavalier puppy's diet for any reason it should be done gradually, over a period of several meals and a few days. Begin by adding a tablespoon or two of the new food, gradually increasing the amount until the meal consists entirely of the new product.

By the time your Cavalier is 10 to 12 months old you can reduce feedings to one or at the most two a day. The main meal can be given either in the morning or evening. It is really a matter of choice on your part. There are two important things to remember: Feed the main meal at the same time every day and make sure what you feed is nutritionally complete.

The single meal can be supplemented by a morning or nighttime snack of hard dog biscuits made especially for small dogs. These biscuits not only become highly anticipated treats to your Cavalier but also are genuinely helpful in maintaining healthy gums and teeth. There seems to

Always make sure that there is plenty of fresh water available at all times, especially to accompany your Cavalier's meal.

A nutritious diet will be evident in your dog's shiny coat and overall healthy appearance.

be some correlation between dirty, unkempt, and unhealthy teeth and mitral valve heart disease. We make tooth care a part of our grooming ritual and give further details in the section that covers grooming.

"Balanced" Diets

In order for a canine diet to qualify as "complete and balanced" in the United States, it must meet standards set by the Subcommittee on Canine Nutrition of the National Research Council of the National Academy of Sciences. Most commercial foods manufactured for dogs meet these standards and prove this by listing the ingredients contained in the food on every package or can. The ingredients are listed in descending order with the main ingredient listed first.

Fed with any regularity at all, refined sugars can cause your Cavalier to become obese and will definitely create tooth decay. Candy stores do not exist in nature and canine teeth are not genetically disposed to handling sugars. Do not feed your Cavalier candy or sweets and avoid products that contain sugar to any high degree.

Fresh water and a properly prepared, balanced diet containing the essential nutrients in correct proportions are all a healthy Cavalier needs to be offered. Dog foods come canned, dry, semi-moist, "scientifically fortified," and "all-natural." A visit to your local supermarket or pet store will reveal the vast array from which you can select. Pet stores usually carry the more premier brands of food that a breeder will most likely recommend.

It is important to remember that all dogs, whether toy or giant, are carnivorous (meat-eating) animals. While the vegetable content of the Cavalier diet should not be overlooked, a dog's physiology

Choose a dog food that is specially formulated for your Cavalier's stage of life and activity level.

Treats and bones can be used as a reward during training sessions.

and anatomy are based upon carnivorous food acquisition. Protein and fat are absolutely essential to the well-being of your Cavalier. In fact, it is wise to add a few drops of vegetable oil or bacon drippings to your dog's diet, particularly during the winter months in colder climates.

Read the list of ingredients of the dog food you buy. Animal protein should appear first on the label's list of ingredients. A base of quality kibble to which meat and even table scraps has been added can provide a nutritious meal for your Cavalier.

This having been said, it should be realized that in the wild, carnivores eat the entire beast they capture and kill. The carnivore's kills consist almost entirely of herbivorous (plant-eating) animals and invariably the carnivore begins its meal with the contents of the herbivore's stomach. This provides the carbohydrates, minerals, and nutrients present in vegetables.

Through centuries of domestication we have made our dogs entirely dependent upon us for their well-being. Therefore we are responsible for duplicating the food balance that the wild dog finds in nature. The domesticated dog's diet must include protein, carbohydrates, fats, roughage, and small amounts of essential minerals and vitamins.

Finding commercially prepared diets that contain all the necessary nutrients will not present a problem. It is important to understand that these commercially prepared foods do contain most of the nutrients your Cavalier requires. Still, most Cavalier breeders recommend vitamin supplementation for a healthy coat and increased stamina, especially for show dogs, pregnant bitches, or very young puppies.

Oversupplementation

A great deal of controversy exists today regarding the orthopedic problems that afflict many breeds. Some claim these problems are entirely hereditary conditions, but many others feel that they can be exacerbated by the overuse of mineral and vitamin supplements for puppies. Over-supplementation is now looked upon by some breeders as a major contributor to many skeletal abnormalities found in the purebred dogs of the day. In giving vitamin supplementation one should *never* exceed the prescribed amount. No vitamin, however, is a substitute for a nutritious balanced diet.

Pregnant and lactating bitches do require supplementation of some kind but here again, it is not a case of "if a little is good, a lot would be a great deal better." Extreme caution is advised in this case and best discussed with your veterinarian.

If the owner of a Cavalier normally eats healthy nutritious food, there is no reason why their dog cannot be given some table scraps. What could possibly be harmful in good nutritious food?

Puppies receive the nutrients they require from nursing, but once weaned, you are responsible for meeting their nutritional needs.

Table scraps should be given only as part of the dog's meal and never from the table. A Cavalier that becomes accustomed to being hand fed from the table can quickly become a real pest at mealtime. The fed-from-the-table Cavalier can decide that is how and only how it wants to eat.

Dogs do not care if food looks like a hot dog or a piece of cheese. Truly nutritious dog foods are seldom manufactured to look like food that appeals to humans. Dogs only care about how food smells and tastes. It is highly doubtful you will be eating your dog's food so do not waste your money on these "looks just like" products.

Be careful when choosing a dog food because some brands contain dyes that may stain your Cavalier's face.

Along these lines, most of the moist or canned foods that have the look of "delicious red beef" look that way because they usually contain great amounts of red dye. They should not be fed to a Cavalier! The same coloring that makes these products look red can stain and discolor the Cavalier's hair. Some breeders claim these products can also cause tearing, which could stain the face of your Cavalier and detract from that lovely expression.

To test the dye content of either canned or dry foods, place a small amount of the moistened food after it has been prepared for your dog on an absorbent towel and allow it to remain there for several hours. If the paper is stained, you can rest assured your dog's hair can be stained as well. Further, preservatives and dyes are no better for your dog than they are for you.

Special Diets

There are now any number of commercially prepared diets for dogs with special dietary needs. The overweight, underweight, or

It is alright to give your Cavalier treats as long as they are nutritious and do not upset his regular diet.

geriatric dog can have his nutritional needs met, as can puppies and growing dogs. The calorie content of these foods is adjusted accordingly. With the correct amount of the right foods and the proper amount of exercise, your Cavalier should stay in top shape. Again, common sense must prevail. Too many calories will increase weight. Reducing calories reduces weight.

Occasionally, a young Cavalier going through the teething period will become a poor eater. The concerned owner's first response is to tempt the dog by hand-feeding special treats and foods that the problem eater seems to prefer. This practice only serves to compound the problem. Once the dog learns to play the waiting game, he will turn up his nose at anything other than his favorite food, knowing full well what he *wants* to eat will eventually arrive.

Unlike humans, dogs have no suicidal tendencies. A healthy dog will not starve himself to death. He may not eat enough to keep him in the shape we find ideal and attractive, but he will definitely eat enough to maintain himself. If your Cavalier is not eating properly and appears to be too thin, it is probably best to consult your veterinarian.

Special Needs of the Cavalier

Exercise

The Cavalier benefits from adequate exercise. The Cavalier, especially if neutered, tends to gain weight with age, particularly if he is allowed to become sedentary.

The breed standard states that the show Cavalier should ideally weigh between 13 and 18 pounds. Naturally, weights can vary above and below these ideal limits depending upon the size and structure of the individual dog. The important thing is to keep your dog trim and fit.

Properly supervised exercise—brisk walking, ball playing, playing with children and other small dogs—are all things that your Cavalier can enjoy and benefit from. Naturally, common sense must be used to the extent and intensity of the exercise you give your Cavalier.

Remember, young puppies have short bursts of energy and then require long rest periods. No puppy should be forced to accompany you on extended walks. Serious injuries can result. Again, short exercise periods and long rest stops for any Cavalier under 10 or 12 months of age. On the other hand, most adult Cavaliers will willingly walk as far as the average owner is inclined to go.

Hot Weather

Caution must be exercised in hot weather. Plan your walks, if you are going to take one, for the first thing in the morning

Do not forget that your Cavalier puppy requires a healthy amount of exercise. One way to get exercise is from vigorous play sessions with other pups.

if at all possible. If you cannot arrange to do this, wait until the sun has set and the outdoor temperature has dropped to a comfortable degree.

You must *never* leave your Cavalier in a car in hot weather. Temper–atures can soar in a matter of minutes and your dog can die of heat exhaustion in less time than you would ever imagine. Rolling down the windows helps little and is dangerous in that an overheated Cavalier will panic and could attempt to escape through the open window. A word to the wise—leave your dog at home in a cool room on hot days.

There is nothing a Cavalier loves more than socializing with people—especially children!

Wet Weather

Do not allow your Cavalier to remain wet if the two of you get caught in the rain in cold weather. At the very least you should thoroughly towel-dry the wet Cavalier. Better still, use your blow dryer (set on medium) to make sure your dog is thoroughly dry and mat free as indicated in the section on bathing and grooming.

Get your Cavalier puppy used to his new leash by attaching it to his collar and giving him some time to get accustomed to the new addition.

Socialization

The Cavalier is by nature a happy dog and takes most situations in stride, but it is important to accommodate the breed's natural instincts by making sure your dog is accustomed to everyday events of all kinds. Traffic, strange noises, loud or hyperactive children, and strange animals can be very intimidating to a dog of any breed that has never experienced them before. Gently and gradually introduce your puppy to as many strange situations as you possibly can.

Make it a practice to take your Cavalier with you whenever practical. The breed is a real crowd pleaser and you will find your Cavalier will savor all the attention he gets.

GROOMING Your Cavalier King Charles Spaniel

REGULAR COAT CARE

A good part of what makes the Cavalier the attractive breed we know is his beautiful silky coat. Although the Cavalier is certainly not a high-maintenance breed, he will only have that special look as long as you are diligent in keeping his coat clean and mat free.

This cannot be accomplished by occasional attacks on the problem after long periods of neglect. The damage done by neglecting the Cavalier coat can normally only be undone by cutting away the accumulated mats. Allowing this to happen is neither attractive nor is it good for your dog. If you are not willing to put in the small amount of time and effort necessary to maintain the Cavalier coat, why not get a smooth-coated dog instead?

A regular grooming regimen will keep your Cavalier looking his best and will allow you to keep on top of any skin or coat problems.

It's never too early to start table training your puppy, whether the youngster is destined for a show career or to help you through the grooming process.

The show Cavalier is not trimmed in any fashion. If your dog is not being shown and is kept only as a pet, it is permissible and helpful to neaten up the long hair on the feet (slippers). This will also help you in seeing to it that the nails are kept short.

Puppy Coat

Undoubtedly the breeder from whom you purchased your Cavalier will have begun to accustom the puppy to grooming as soon as there was enough hair to brush. You must continue with grooming sessions or begin them at once if, for some reason, they have not been started.

The first piece of equipment you should obtain is a grooming table. A grooming table can either be built or purchased at your local pet emporium. Even a sturdy card table topped with a non-skid pad can be used just so long as it is steady and does not wobble or shake. An unsteady table is a frightening thing for any dog.

Make sure that whatever kind of table you use it is of a height at which you can work comfortably. Adjustable-height grooming tables are available at most pet shops.

You will also need to invest in a brush for long-haired dogs, a steel comb, barber's scissors, and a pair of nail clippers. Also very useful is a quality spray-type coat conditioner for a finishing touch after your dog is thoroughly brushed. Consider the fact you will be using these grooming tools for many years to come, so buy the best of these items that you can afford.

The brushes that you will need are a pin brush (sometimes called a Poodle brush) and a good bristle brush. Another popular brush that can be used is called a slicker brush. The slicker brush must be used very carefully, however, or it will pull out your dog's coat rather than simply untangle it. All these tools can be purchased at your local pet shop or at any dog show.

Do not attempt to groom your puppy on the floor. The puppy will only attempt to get away from you when he has decided enough is enough, and you will spend a good part of your time chasing the puppy around the room. Nor is sitting on the floor for long stretches of time the most comfortable position in the world for the average adult.

There is very little hair to brush and comb on a Cavalier puppy, but do not delay in teaching your puppy to behave during those early grooming sessions. Maturity will bring a great deal more hair to deal with.

Nail Trimming

This is a good time to accustom your Cavalier to having his nails trimmed and his feet inspected. Always inspect your dog's feet for cracked pads. If your Cavalier accompanies you to the park or woods, check between the toes for splinters and thorns. Pay particular attention to any swollen or tender areas.

The nails of the Cavalier that spends most of his time indoors or on grass when outdoors can grow long very quickly. Do not allow the nails to become overgrown and then expect to cut them back easily. Each nail has a blood vessel running through the center called the quick. The quick grows close to the end of the nail and contains very sensitive nerve endings. If the nail is allowed to grow too long it will be impossible to cut it back to a proper length without cutting into the quick. This causes severe pain to the dog and can also result in a great deal of bleeding that can be very difficult to stop.

Should the quick be nipped in the trimming process, however, there are many blood clotting products available at pet shops that will almost immediately stem the flow of blood. It is wise to have one of these products on hand in case there is a nail trimming accident or the dog tears a nail on his own.

As soon as your Cavalier puppy is old enough, begin getting him used to having his nails trimmed and feet inspected. This will make the job easier as he gets older.

Caring for the Teeth

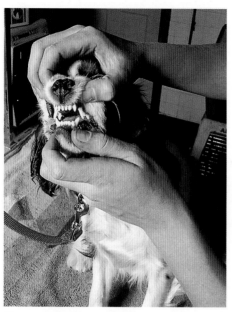

As previously mentioned, in our experience mitral valve heart disease seems to be somehow correlated to unhealthy teeth and gums. It is imperative that a Cavalier's teeth be kept clean. Daily brushing or frequent tooth scaling at home is absolutely mandatory. Your veterinarian will be glad to clean your dog's teeth on a regular basis. Use grooming time to carefully inspect your dog's teeth, as tartar can build up very quickly.

Use grooming time to inspect your Cavalier's teeth, as early detection can prevent dental problems. Brushing his teeth regularly and giving him chew toys can help.

Cavaliers normally have a full complement of 42 teeth that can make for crowding in the mouth of a small breed like this one. This makes the breed susceptible to accumulation of debris in the mouth. Only regular dental care can prevent mouth problems. It is always wise to put the Cavalier on an antibiotic if any serious cleaning or dental work is done by your veterinarian as the bacteria released into the mouth can lead to heart disease.

Ears

As is the case with any breed that has hanging ears, the insides of your Cavalier's ears must be kept clean. Wax, mites, yeast, or other infections can easily build up if regular care is not taken. If the insides of the ears look dirty or have an odor, they must be cleaned. You can use a moist, soapy washcloth to do this but, if you do, thoroughly rinse all the soap out when you are done.

Alcohol or an ear-cleaning product from your veterinarian on a cotton swab can also be used, but in doing so, never probe further into the ear than the area you can see. If you are keeping the ears clean and they still have an odor or discharge, alert your veterinarian at once. Cavalier ears can become infected overnight and vigilance is the only thing that will keep them clean and healthy.

Eyes

Cavalier eyes can tear profusely during teething and in pollen season. If tearing does not clear up, have your veterinarian check to see if there might be clogged tear ducts or an eye infection. There are several tear-cleansing products on the market that can be used but none of them will work as well as simply keeping the eyes healthy.

BATHING

Bathe your Cavalier whenever needed. Use a quality shampoo made especially for dogs as these products have the proper pH balance. Keep a good conditioner on the coat to cut down on any

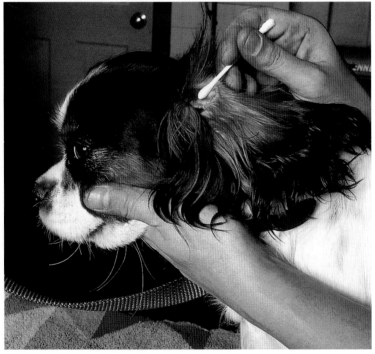

You may use a cotton swab to help keep your Cavalier's ears clean.

tangles and knots. A Cavalier should never be bathed until after he has been thoroughly brushed. If all mats are not out before you bathe, they will only get worse when doused with water.

A small cotton ball placed inside each ear will prevent water from running down into the dog's ear canal. A drop or two of clean mineral oil or a dab of petroleum jelly kept just for that purpose can be placed on the rim of each eye to avoid shampoo irritation.

A rubber mat should be placed at the bottom of the tub so that your dog does not slip and become frightened. A rubber spray hose is absolutely necessary to remove all shampoo residue. Rinse thoroughly, apply a quality coat conditioner, and rinse again.

In bathing, start behind the ears and work back, massaging the suds in thoroughly. Finally, carefully wash around the face with a soft cloth, being very careful not to get suds into your dog's eyes. Rinse well and when you are sure you have removed all shampoo

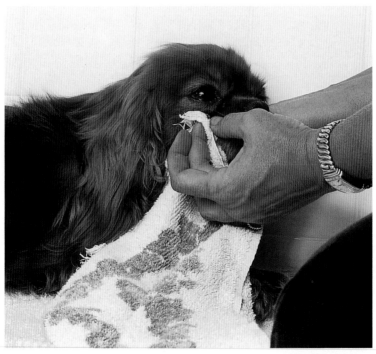

Before bathing your Cavalier, a dab of mineral oil or petroleum jelly should prevent shampoo suds from irritating his eyes.

Good oral health is important to your Cavalier's well-being.

residue, rinse once more. Shampoo residue in the coat is sure to dry the hair and could cause skin irritation.

As soon as you have completed the bath use a heavy towel to remove as much of the excess water as possible. Your Cavalier will undoubtedly assist you in the process by shaking a great deal of the water out of the coat on his own.

Using a Hair Dryer

It helps to gently "brush dry" your Cavalier using your pin brush and a hair dryer. Do not leave a Cavalier in a cage with a cage dryer. This causes the coat to stand away from the body rather than have the straight silky look, which is proper. Always set your hair dryer at medium setting, never hot. The hot setting may be quicker but it will also dry out the hair and could easily burn the delicate skin of your Cavalier.

Keep the ears clean by putting a little ear cleanser in the ear and wiping it with a tissue. Do not probe into the ear beyond where you can see! The delicate eardrum can be easily injured. If you suspect a problem further down in the ear canal, consult your veterinarian.

HOUSETRAINING and Training Your Cavalier

THOUGHTS ON TRAINING

All dogs can be trained. It does appear that some breeds are more difficult to get the desired response from than others. Usually though, this has more to do with the trainer and his or her training methods than with the dog's inability to learn. With the proper approach, any dog that is not mentally deficient can be taught to be a good canine citizen. Many dog owners do not understand how a dog learns, nor do they realize they can be breed-specific in their approach to training.

Young Cavalier puppies have an amazing capacity to learn. This capacity is greater than most humans realize. It is important to remember though, these young puppies also forget with great speed unless they are reminded of what they have learned by continual reinforcement. It is also critical that training be approached in a firm and gentle manner. The Cavalier does not respond to harsh treatment or heavy hands.

As puppies leave the nest they began their search for two things: a pack leader and the rules set down by that leader by which the

One must remember that a Cavalier has an enormous capacity to learn and loves to please his master.

As a pack animal, a new puppy will look for the leader in the home. If he doesn't find one, he will take over the role himself.

puppies can abide. Because puppies, particularly Cavalier puppies, are cuddly, cute, and very small, their owners fail miserably in supplying these very basic needs of every dog. Instead, the owner immediately begins to respond to the demands of the puppy.

For example, a puppy quickly learns he will be allowed into the house or a room because he is barking or whining, not because he can only enter the house when he is *not* barking or whining. Instead of learning that the only way he will be fed is to follow a set procedure (i.e., sitting or lying down on command) he learns leaping about the kitchen or barking incessantly is what gets results.

If the young puppy cannot find his pack leader in an owner the puppy assumes the role of pack leader. Yes, even as small as that bit of fluff is, if there are no rules imposed, the Cavalier puppy learns to make his own rules. And unfortunately, the negligent owner continually reinforces the puppy's decisions by allowing him to govern the household.

With small dogs like our Cavalier, this scenario can produce a neurotic nuisance. In large dogs the situation can be downright dangerous. Neither situation is an acceptable one.

The key to successful training lies in establishing the proper relationship between dog and owner. The owner or the owning family must be the pack leader and the individual or family must provide the rules by which the dog abides.

Once this is established, ease of training largely depends on just how much a dog depends upon his master's approval. The entirely dependent dog lives to please his master and will do everything in his power to evoke the approval response from the person to whom he is devoted.

At the opposite end of the pole we have the totally independent dog that is not remotely concerned with what his master thinks or wants. Dependency varies from one breed to the next and, to a degree, within breeds as well. Cavaliers are no exception to this rule. Fortunately for the owner of a Cavalier, this breed really wants to please.

HOUSETRAINING

The Crate Method

A major key to successfully training your Cavalier, whether it is obedience training or housebreaking, is *avoidance.* It is much easier for your Cavalier to learn something if you do not first have to have him unlearn bad habits. The crate training method of housebreaking is a highly successful method of avoiding bad habits before they begin.

First-time Cavalier owners or those who have never attempted to use the crate method are inclined to initially see it as cruel, but those same people will return later and thank us profusely for having suggested it in the first place. They are also surprised to find that the

Choose the puppy in the litter that best responds to you and fits your personality.

Make sure your Cavalier has plenty of time outside during the housetraining process.

puppy will eventually come to think of his crate as a place of private retreat—a den to which he will retreat for rest and privacy. The success of the crate method is based upon the fact that puppies will not soil the area in which they sleep unless they are forced to.

Use of a cage reduces housetraining time to an absolute minimum. It also avoids keeping a puppy under constant stress by incessantly correcting him for making mistakes in the house. The anti-cage advocates consider it cruel to confine a puppy for any length of time but find no problem in constantly harassing and punishing the puppy because he has wet on the carpet or relieved himself behind the sofa.

Crates come in a wide variety of styles. The fiberglass shipping kennels used by many airlines are popular with Cavalier owners but residents of the extremely warm climates sometimes prefer the wire cage type. Both are available at pet stores.

The crate used for housebreaking should only be large enough for the puppy to stand, lie down, and stretch out comfortably. There are many sizes to choose from. We advise using the medium-size, airline-type crate, approximately 20 inches high by 24 inches wide by 30 inches long. This size seems ideal for most Cavaliers. It is, of course, larger than what is required for the three-month-old puppy but this can be handled easily by blocking off excess space with a plywood barrier.

Make sure your Cavaliers are in a safe, partitioned-off area when left unsupervised.

As soon as your Cavalier puppy finishes his meal, immediately take him outside to the spot where you want him to learn to relieve himself.

Begin to feed your puppy in the crate. Keep the door closed and latched while the puppy is eating. When the meal is finished, open the cage and *carry* your puppy outdoors to the spot where you want him to learn to eliminate. In the event you do not have outdoor access or will be away from home for long periods of time, begin housebreaking by placing newspapers in an out of the way corner that is easily accessible for the puppy. If you consistently take your puppy to the same spot, you will reinforce the habit of going there for that purpose. You will have to be especially diligent with most Cavaliers during inclement weather. A Cavalier puppy may well prefer to take care of his duties inside the warm house rather than outdoors.

It is important that you do not let the puppy loose after eating. Young puppies will eliminate almost immediately after eating or drinking. They will also be ready to relieve themselves when they first wake up, as well as after playing. If you keep a watchful eye on your puppy you will quickly learn when this is about to take place.

Stick to a regular schedule by taking your dog for walks every day at the same time.

A puppy usually circles and sniffs the floor just before he will relieve himself. Do not give your puppy an opportunity to learn that he can eliminate in the house! Your housetraining chores will be reduced considerably if you avoid this in the first place.

If you are not able to watch your puppy every minute, he should be in his crate with the door securely latched. Each time you put your puppy in the crate, give him a small treat of some kind. Throw the treat to the back of the crate and encourage the puppy to walk in on his own. When he does so, praise the puppy and perhaps hand him another piece of the treat through the opening in the front of the crate.

Do not succumb to your puppy's complaints about being in his crate. The puppy must learn to stay there and to do so without complaining. A quick "no" command and a tap on the crate will usually get the puppy to understand that his theatrics will not result in liberation. (Remember, as the pack leader you make the rules and the puppy must learn what they are!)

Do understand a Cavalier puppy of 8 to 12 weeks will not be able to contain himself for long periods of time. Puppies of that age must relieve themselves every few hours, except at night. Your schedule must be adjusted accordingly. Also make sure your puppy has relieved himself—both bowel and bladder—the last thing at night and do not dawdle when you wake up in the morning.

Your first priority in the morning is to get the puppy outdoors. Just how early this ritual takes place will undoubtedly depend much more upon your puppy than on you. If your Cavalier is like most others there will be no doubt in your mind when he needs to be let out. You will also very quickly learn to tell the difference between the "this is an emergency" complaint and the "I just want out" grumbling. Do not test the young puppy's ability to contain himself. His vocal demands to be let out will confirm that the housebreaking lesson is being learned.

If you find it necessary to be away from home all day, you should not leave your puppy in a crate. On the other hand, do not make the mistake of allowing him to roam the house, or even a large room, at will. Confine the puppy to a small room or partitioned-off area and cover the floor with newspaper. Make this area large enough so that the puppy will not have to relieve himself next to his bed, food, or water bowl. You will soon find the puppy will be inclined to use one particular spot to perform his bowel and bladder functions. When you are home you must take the puppy to this exact spot to eliminate at the appropriate time.

BASIC TRAINING

Never begin training when you are irritated, distressed, or preoccupied. Nor should you begin basic training in a place that will

Both you and your puppy should be in the proper mood to begin a training session. Make sure there are no distractions and that you are concentrating on the task at hand.

Start training your Cavalier puppy early; a well-trained dog will make friends easily.

interfere with you or your dog's concentration. At first, the two of you should work in a place where you can concentrate fully upon each other. Once the commands are understood and learned you can begin testing your dog in public places.

It is best to start a Cavalier's general basic training at four to six months. Before that time, the puppy's concentration span is minimal and forcing him to obey can be traumatic.

Cavaliers respond well to lots of praise but do not respond to yelling or being struck. Never resort to shaking or striking your Cavalier puppy. A very stern "no!" is usually more than sufficient and even with

Your puppy should get accustomed to a soft, lightweight collar first, then let him get used to the feeling of something attached to his collar before you proceed with leash training.

the most persistent unwanted behavior, striking the ground with a rolled-up newspaper is about as extreme as you will ever need to be.

The No! Command

There is no doubt whatsoever that one of the most important commands your Cavalier puppy will ever learn is the meaning of the no! command. There is no need to wait. The puppy can begin to learn this command just as soon as he is comfortably situated in your home.

One important piece of advice in using this and all other commands—*never give a command you are not prepared and able to enforce!* A good leader does not enforce rules arbitrarily. The only way a puppy learns to obey commands is to realize that once issued, commands must be complied.

Be fair to your dog. He can easily learn the difference between things he can and cannot do. A dog is not able to learn that there are some things he can do one time but not the next. Yelling at your dog for lying on the bed (which most Cavaliers assume is their birthright) one day and not the next serves only to confuse.

Leash Training

Begin leash training by putting a soft lightweight collar on your puppy. After a few hours of occasional scratching at the unaccustomed addition your puppy will quickly forget it is even there.

It may not be necessary for the puppy or adult Cavalier to wear his collar and identification tags within the confines of your home. No Cavalier, however, should leave home without a collar and the attached leash held securely in your hand.

Get your puppy accustomed to his collar by leaving it on for a few minutes at a time. Gradually extend the time you leave the collar on. Once this is accomplished, attach a lightweight leash to the collar while you are playing with the puppy. Do not try to guide the puppy at first. You are only trying to get the puppy used to having something attached to the collar.

To get your puppy to follow you as you move around, coax him along with a treat of some kind. Let the puppy smell what you have in your hand and then move a few steps back holding the treat in front of the puppy's nose. Just as the puppy takes a few steps toward you, praise him enthusiastically and continue to do so as you move along.

Make the first few lessons brief and fun for the puppy. Continue the lessons in your home or yard until the puppy is completely unconcerned about the fact that he is on a leash. With a treat in one hand and the leash in the other, you can begin to use both to guide the puppy in the direction you wish to go. Eventually the two of you can venture out on the sidewalk in front of your house and then on to adventures everywhere! This is one lesson no puppy is too young to learn.

The Come Command

The next most important lesson for the Cavalier puppy to learn is to come when called. Therefore, it is important that the puppy learn his name as soon as possible. Constant repetition is what does the trick in teaching a puppy his name. Use the name every time you talk to your puppy. Talk to your dog. There is a quotation we particularly like that appeared in an old British dog book we found regarding conversations with our canine friends. It states simply, "Of course you should talk to your dogs. But talk sense!"

Learning to come on command could save your dog's life when the two of you venture out into the world. "Come" is the command that a dog must understand he has to obey without question, but the dog should not associate that command with fear. Your dog's response to his name and the word "come" should always be associated with a pleasant experience such as great praise and petting or even a food treat.

Again, remember it is much easier to avoid the establishment of bad habits than it is to correct them once set. *Never* give the come command unless you are sure your puppy will come to you.

The very young puppy is far more inclined to respond to the come command than the older dog. Young puppies are entirely dependent upon you. An older Cavalier may well lose some of that dependency, especially if a bird flutters by or some other creature darts ahead. Cavaliers can become terribly preoccupied with their surroundings. So start your come-on-command training early on.

Use the command initially when the puppy is already on his way to you or give the command while walking or running away from the youngster. Clap your hands and sound very happy and excited about having the puppy join in on this "game."

The very young Cavalier puppy will normally want to stay as close to his owner as possible, especially in strange surroundings. When your puppy sees you moving away, his natural inclination

Don't spend too much time on any one training session. Make each session brief and fun for your Cavalier—and for you!

will be to get close to you. This is a perfect time to use the come command.

You may want to attach a long leash or light rope to the puppy's collar to ensure the correct response. Do not chase or punish your puppy for not obeying the come command. Doing so in the initial stages of training makes the youngster associate the command with something to fear and this will result in avoidance rather than the immediate positive response you desire. It is imperative that you praise your Cavalier puppy lavishly and give him a treat when he does come to you, even if he delays responding for many minutes.

The Sit and Stay Commands

Just as important to your Cavalier puppy's safety as the no! command and learning to come when called are the sit and stay commands. Even a very young Cavalier can learn the sit command quickly, especially if it appears to be a game and a food treat is involved.

First, remember the Cavalier-in-training should always be on collar and leash for all his lessons. A Cavalier puppy is curious about everything that goes on around him and is not beyond getting up and walking away when he has decided he needs to investigate something.

Give the sit command just before you reach down and exert light pressure on your puppy's rear. Praise the puppy profusely when he does sit, even though it was you who made the effort. A food treat

When your puppy obeys the come command, praise him profusely and give him a treat.

of some kind always seems to make the experience that much more enjoyable for the puppy.

Continue holding the puppy's rear end down and repeat the sit command several times. If your puppy makes an attempt to get up, repeat the command yet again while exerting light pressure on the rear end until the correct position is assumed. Make your puppy stay in this position a little bit longer with each succeeding lesson. Begin with a few seconds and increase the time as the

The sit command is the foundation for your Cavalier's training.

lessons progress over the following weeks.

Should your puppy attempt to get up or lie down he should be corrected by simply saying, "sit!" in a firm voice. This should be accompanied by returning the dog to the desired position. Only when *you* decide your dog should get up should he be allowed to do so. Do not test the extent of your young Cavalier puppy's patience. Remember you are dealing with a baby and the attention span of any youngster is relatively limited.

When you do decide the dog may get up, call his name, say "OK," and make a big fuss over him. Praise and a food treat are in order every time your Cavalier responds correctly.

Once your puppy has mastered the sit lesson you may start on the stay command. With your Cavalier on leash and facing you, command him to sit, then take a step or two backward. If your dog attempts to get up to follow, firmly say, "sit, stay!" While you are saying this, raise your hand, palm toward the dog, and again command, "stay!"

If your dog attempts to get up, you must correct him at once, returning him to the sit position and repeating, "stay!" Once your Cavalier begins to understand what you want, you can gradually increase the distance you step back. With a long leash attached to your dog's collar, start with a few steps and gradually increase the distance to several yards. It is important for your Cavalier to learn that the sit, stay command must be obeyed no matter how far away you are. With age and advanced training, your Cavalier can be taught that the command is to be obeyed even when you leave the room or are entirely out of sight.

As your Cavalier becomes accustomed to responding to this lesson and is able to remain in the sit position for as long as you command, do not end the command by calling the dog to you. Walk back to your dog and say "OK." This will let your dog know the command is over. When your Cavalier becomes entirely dependable in this lesson you can then call the dog to you.

The sit, stay command can take considerable time and patience to get across to puppies. You must not forget their attention span will be short. Keep the stay part of the lesson very short until your puppy is at least six months old.

The Down Command

Do not try and teach your puppy too many things at once. Wait until you have mastered one lesson quite well before moving on to something new. When you feel quite confident that your puppy is comfortable with the sit and stay commands, you can start work on down. This is the single word command for lie down. Use the down command *only* when you want the dog to lie down. If you want your Cavalier to get off your sofa or to stop jumping up on people, use the off command. Do not interchange these two commands. Doing so will only serve to confuse your dog and evoking the right response will become next to impossible.

The down position is especially useful if you want your Cavalier to remain in one place for a long period of time. Most dogs are far more inclined to stay put when lying down than when they are sitting or standing.

Teaching this command to your Cavalier may take more time and patience than the previous lessons the two of you have undertaken. It is believed by some animal behaviorists that assuming the down position somehow represents greater submissiveness.

With your Cavalier sitting in front of and facing you, hold a treat in your right hand with the excess part of the leash in your left hand. Hold the treat under the dog's nose and slowly bring your hand

Once the puppy understands what is required of him when told to "stay," you can increase the distance to which you step away from him.

With patience, persistence, and praise, your Cavalier will eagerly learn what you want to teach him.

down to the ground. Your dog will follow the treat with his head and neck. As he does, give the down command and exert *light* pressure on the dog's shoulders with your left hand. If your dog resists the pressure on his shoulders *do not continue pushing down.* Doing so will only create more resistance. Reach down and slide the dog's feet toward you until he is lying down.

An alternative method of getting your Cavalier headed into the down position is to move around to the dog's right side and, as you draw his attention downward with your right hand, slide your left hand under the dog's front legs and gently slide them forward. You will undoubtedly have to be on your knees next to the youngster in order to do this. As your dog's forelegs begin to slide out to his front, keep moving the treat along the ground until the dog's whole body is lying on the ground while you continually repeat, "down."

Once your dog has assumed the position you desire, give him the treat and a lot of praise. Continue assisting your Cavalier into the down position until he does so on his own. Be firm and be patient.

The Heel Command

In learning to heel, your Cavalier will walk on your left side with his shoulder next to your leg no matter which direction you might go or how quickly you turn. Learning this command can be an extremely valuable lesson for your dog, even though he is a toy breed. A Cavalier that darts back and forth in front of or under his master's feet can endanger himself and cause serious injury to his owner as well.

Teaching your Cavalier to heel is critical to off-leash control and will not only make your daily walks far more enjoyable, it will make for a more tractable companion when the two of you are in crowded or confusing situations. We do not recommend ever allowing your Cavalier to be off leash when you are away from home, but it is important to know you can control your dog no matter what the circumstances.

A lightweight, link-chain collar is best to use for the heeling lesson and changing to this collar for the lesson indicates what you are doing is "business" and not just a casual walk. These link-chain collars provide both quick pressure around the neck and the chain itself makes a snapping sound. These things will assist in getting the dog's attention. The collars are sometimes called "choke collars," but rest assured that when properly used they will not choke the dog. The pet shop in which you buy the collar will assist you in learning how to properly place the collar around your dog's neck.

When you begin your puppy's early leash training, you should accustom the youngster to walk on your left side. The leash should

In the correct down position, your Cavalier's body should be completely flat on the ground.

cross your body from the dog's collar to your right hand. The excess portion of the leash will be folded into your right hand and your left hand will be used to make corrections with the leash.

For the heeling lesson, a quick, gentle jerk on the leash with your left hand will keep your dog from lunging side to side, pulling ahead, or darting between your legs. As you make a correction give the heel command. Keep the leash loose when your dog maintains the proper position at your side.

If your dog begins to drift away give the leash a quick jerk, guide the dog back to the correct position, and give the heel command. Do not pull on the lead with steady pressure. What is needed is a sharp but gentle jerking motion to get your dog's attention.

TRAINING CLASSES

There are few limits to what a patient, consistent Cavalier owner can teach his or her dog. Don't forget the breed's long history of human association and eagerness to please. Once lessons are mastered you will find that most Cavaliers will perform with the enthusiasm and gusto that make all the hard work well worthwhile.

For advanced obedience work beyond the basics it is wise for the Cavalier owner to consider local professional assistance. Professional trainers have had long-standing experience in avoiding the pitfalls of obedience training and can help you to avoid them as well.

This training assistance can be obtained in many ways. Classes are particularly good in that your dog will learn to obey commands

It might take a while for your young Cavalier puppy to get used to training sessions, but with time he will soon enjoy the hours you spend together.

Training your Cavalier will bring the two of you closer than ever before as your puppy aims to please you.

in spite of all the interesting sights and smells of other dogs. There are free-of-charge classes at many parks and recreation facilities, as well as very formal and sometimes very expensive individual lessons with private trainers.

There are also some obedience schools that will take your Cavalier and train him for you. However, unless your schedule provides no time at all to train your dog, having someone else train the dog for you would be last on our list of recommendations. The rapport that develops between the owner who has trained his or her Cavalier and the dog himself is incomparable. The effort you expend as you teach your dog to be a pleasant companion and good canine citizen pays off in years of enjoyable companionship.

Versatility

The Cavalier is an extremely versatile breed and there is no end to the number of activities you and your pet can enjoy together. The breed is highly successful in both conformation shows and obedience trials.

There are Canine Good Citizen certificates that can be earned through the American Kennel Club, and a new event called agility trials. The agility trials are actually obstacle courses for dogs, but Cavalier owners find that their little dogs enjoy these exercises as much as they do.

The well-trained Cavalier will be a joy for years to come.

Neither should you forget that a good many Cavaliers retain their hunting instinct and can provide the outdoorsman with a great deal of pleasure in pursuing hunting titles and championships. Even if you do not hunt, a day tramping in the field can be a most healthful and enjoyable pastime.

Owners not inclined toward competitive events might find enjoyment in having their Cavalier serve as a therapy dog. Dogs used in this area are trained to assist the sick, the elderly, and often the handicapped. The people love the Cavalier's wistful and affectionate personality and the dogs themselves seem particularly suited to this kind of work because they are gentle and quiet. Cavaliers have also proven themselves to be of outstanding assistance to the hearing impaired by signaling their owners at the sound of the phone, the doorbell, or the sound of someone knocking or calling. This can be a wonderful addition to someone's life.

The well-trained Cavalier can provide a wealth of both indoor and outdoor activities for the owner. You are limited only by the amount of time you wish to invest in this remarkable breed.

A responsibly bred and well-cared-for Cavalier can be a happy, healthy companion for years. Ch. Wyndcrest Baroque of Rattlebridge, owned by Meredith Johnson-Snyder.

SPORT of Purebred Dogs

Welcome to the exciting and sometimes frustrating sport of dogs. No doubt you are trying to learn more about dogs or you wouldn't be deep into this book. This section covers the basics that may entice you, further your knowledge and help you to understand the dog world.

Dog showing has been a very popular sport for a long time and has been taken quite seriously by some. Others only enjoy it as a hobby.

The Kennel Club in England was formed in 1859, the American Kennel Club was established in 1884 and the Canadian Kennel Club was formed in 1888. The purpose of these clubs was to register purebred dogs and maintain their Stud Books. In the beginning, the concept of registering dogs was not readily accepted. More than 36 million dogs have been enrolled in the AKC Stud Book since its inception in 1888. Presently the kennel clubs not only register dogs but adopt and enforce rules and regulations governing dog shows, obedience trials and field trials. Over the years they have fostered and encouraged interest in the health and welfare of the purebred dog. They routinely donate funds to veterinary research for study on genetic disorders.

Below are the addresses of the kennel clubs in the United States, Great Britain and Canada.

Ch. Grantilley Secret Love at Ambleside—"Katie"—has a perfect Blenheim lozenge on her head and is an excellent example of the breed.

The American Kennel Club
260 Madison Avenue
New York, NY 10016
or 5580 Centerview Drive,
Raleigh, NC 2760

The Kennel Club
1 Clarges Street
Picadilly, London, WIY 8AB, England

The Canadian Kennel Club
89 Skyway Avenue
Etobicoke, Ontario, Canada M9W 6R4

Today there are numerous activities that are enjoyable for both the dog and the handler. Some of the activities include conformation showing, obedience competition, tracking, agility, the Canine Good Citizen Certificate, and a wide range of instinct tests that vary from breed to breed. Where you start depends upon your goals which early on may not be readily apparent.

Puppy Kindergarten

Every puppy will benefit from this class. PKT is the foundation for all future dog activities from conformation to "couch potatoes." Pet owners should make an effort to attend even if they never expect to show their dog. The class is designed for puppies about three months of age with graduation at approxi-mately five months of age. All the puppies will be in the same age group and, even though some may be a little unruly, there should not be any real

Ch. Elvenhome Buckthorn has classic Blenheim colorings and head markings.

problem. This class will teach the puppy some beginning obedience. As in all obedience classes the owner learns how to train his own dog. The PKT class gives the puppy the opportunity to interact with other puppies in the same age group and exposes him to strangers, which is very important. Some dogs grow up with behavior problems, one of them being fear of strangers. As you can see, there can be much to gain from this class.

There are some basic obedience exercises that every dog should learn. Some of these can be started with puppy kindergarten.

CONFORMATION

Conformation showing is our oldest dog show sport. This type of showing is based on the dog's appearance—that is his structure, movement and attitude. When considering this type of showing, you need to be aware of your breed's standard and be able to evaluate your dog compared to that standard. The breeder of your puppy or other experienced breeders would be good sources for such an evaluation. Puppies can go through lots of changes over a period of time. Many puppies start out as promising hopefuls and then after maturing may be disappointing as show candidates. Even so this should not deter them from being excellent pets.

Usually conformation training classes are offered by the local kennel or obedience clubs. These are excellent places for training puppies. The puppy should be able to walk on a lead before entering such a class. Proper ring procedure and technique for posing (stacking) the dog will be demonstrated as well as gaiting the dog. Usually certain patterns are used in the ring such as the triangle or the "L." Conformation class, like the PKT class, will give your youngster the opportunity to socialize with different breeds of dogs and humans too.

It takes some time to learn the routine of conformation showing. Usually one starts at the puppy matches that may be AKC Sanctioned or Fun Matches. These matches are generally for puppies from two or three months to a year old, and there may be classes for the adult over the age of 12 months. Similar to point shows, the classes are divided by sex and after completion of the classes in that breed or variety, the class winners compete for Best of Breed or Variety. The winner goes on to compete in the Group and the Group winners compete for Best in Match. No championship points are awarded for match wins.

A few matches can be great training for puppies even though there is no intention to go on showing. Matches enable the puppy to meet new people and be handled by a stranger—the judge. It is also a change of environment, which broadens the horizon for both dog and handler. Matches and other dog activities boost the confidence of the handler and especially the younger handlers.

Conformation is the oldest dog show sport. It is wholly based on the dog's appearance—his structure, movement, and even his attitude are important.

Earning an AKC championship is built on a point system, which is different from Great Britain. To become an AKC Champion of Record the dog must earn 15 points. The number of points earned each time depends upon the number of dogs in competition. The number of points available at each show depends upon the breed, its sex and the location of the show. The United States is divided into ten AKC zones. Each zone has its own set of points. The purpose of the zones is to try to equalize the points available from breed to breed and area to area. The AKC adjusts the point scale annually.

The number of points that can be won at a show are between one and five. Three-, four- and five-point wins are considered majors. Not only does the dog need 15 points won under three different judges, but those points must include two majors under two different judges. Canada also works on a point system but majors are not required.

Dogs always show before bitches. The classes available to those seeking points are: Puppy (which may be divided into 6 to 9 months and 9 to 12 months); 12 to 18 months; Novice; Bred-by-Exhibitor; American-bred; and Open. The class winners of the same sex of each breed or variety compete against each other for Winners Dog and Winners Bitch. A Reserve Winners Dog and Reserve Winners Bitch are also awarded but do not carry any points unless the

Winners win is disallowed by AKC. The Winners Dog and Bitch compete with the specials (those dogs that have attained championship) for Best of Breed or Variety, Best of Winners and Best of Opposite Sex. It is possible to pick up an extra point or even a major if the points are higher for the defeated winner than those of Best of Winners. The latter would get the higher total from the defeated winner.

At an all-breed show, each Best of Breed or Variety winner will go on to his respective Group and then the Group winners will compete against each other for Best in Show. There are seven Groups: Sporting, Hounds, Working, Terriers, Toys, Non-Sporting and Herding. Obviously there are no Groups at speciality shows (those shows that have only one breed or a show such as the American Spaniel Club's Flushing Spaniel Show, which is for all flushing spaniel breeds).

Earning a championship in England is somewhat different since they do not have a point system. Challenge Certificates are awarded if the judge feels the dog is deserving regardless of the number of dogs in competition. A dog must earn three Challenge Certificates under three different judges, with at least one of these Certificates being won after the age of 12 months. Competition is very strong and entries may be higher than they are in the U.S. The Kennel Club's Challenge Certificates are only available at Championship Shows.

In England, The Kennel Club regulations require that certain dogs, Border Collies and Gundog breeds, qualify in a working capacity (i.e., obedience or field trials) before becoming a full Champion. If they do not qualify in the working aspect, then they are designated a Show Champion, which is equivalent to the AKC's Champion of Record. A Gundog may be granted the title of Field Trial Champion (FT Ch.) if it passes all the tests in the field but would also have to qualify in conformation before becoming a full Champion. A Border Collie that earns the title of Obedience Champion (Ob Ch.) must also qualify in the conformation ring before becoming a Champion.

The U.S. doesn't have a designation full Champion but does award for Dual and Triple Champions. The Dual Champion must be a Champion of Record, and either Champion Tracker, Herding Champion, Obedience Trial Champion or Field Champion. Any dog that has been awarded the titles of Champion of Record, and any two of the following: Champion Tracker, Herding Champion, Obedience Trial Champion or Field Champion, may be designated as a Triple Champion.

The shows in England seem to put more emphasis on breeder judges than those in the U.S. There is much competition within the breeds. Therefore the quality of the individual breeds should be very good. In the United States we tend to have more "all around judges" (those that judge multiple breeds) and use the breeder judges at the specialty shows. Breeder judges are more familiar with their own breed since they are actively breeding that breed or did so at one time. Americans emphasize Group and Best in Show wins and promote them accordingly.

The shows in England can be very large and extend over several days, with the Groups being scheduled on different days. Though multi-day shows are not common in the U.S., there are cluster shows, where several different clubs will use the same show site over consecutive days.

These puppies are all sure to have the deep chestnut red that is so highly desirable in the Blenheim Cavalier.

Westminster Kennel Club is our most prestigious show although the entry is limited to 2500. In recent years, entry has been limited to Champions. This show is more formal than the majority of the shows with the judges wearing formal attire and the handlers fashionably dressed. In most instances the quality of the dogs is superb. After all, it is a show of Champions. It is a good show to study the AKC registered breeds and is by far the most exciting—especially since it is televised! WKC is one of the few shows in this country that is still benched. This means the dog must be in his benched area during the show hours except when he is being groomed, in the ring, or being exercised.

Typically, the handlers are very particular about their appearances. They are careful not to wear something that will detract from their dog but will perhaps enhance it. American ring procedure is quite formal compared to that of other countries. There is a certain etiquette expected between the judge and exhibitor and among the other exhibitors. Of course it is not always the case but the judge is supposed to be polite, not engaging in small talk or acknowledging how well he knows the handler. There is a more informal and relaxed atmosphere at the shows in other countries. For instance, the dress code is more casual. I can see where this might be more fun for the exhibitor and especially for the novice. The U.S. is very

These two Ruby Cavalier King Charles Spaniels are English champions owned by Maureen Milton.

handler-oriented in many of the breeds. It is true, in most instances, that the experienced professional handler can present the dog better and will have a feel for what a judge likes.

In England, Crufts is The Kennel Club's own show and is most assuredly the largest dog show in the world. They've been known to have an entry of nearly 20,000, and the show lasts four days. Entry is only gained by qualifying through winning in specified classes at another Championship Show. Westminster is strictly

Here is a real family of champions—Ch. Wye Rebound of Rattlebridge and Ch. Rattlebridge Rosie O'Grady and their daughter, Rattlebridge Naughty By Nature.

conformation, but Crufts exhibitors and spectators enjoy not only conformation but obedience, agility and a multitude of exhibitions as well. Obedience was admitted in 1957 and agility in 1983.

If you are handling your own dog, please give some consideration to your apparel. For sure the dress code at matches is more informal than the point shows. However, you should wear something a little more appropriate than beach attire or ragged jeans and bare feet. If you check out the handlers and see what is presently fashionable, you'll catch on. Men usually dress with a shirt and tie and a nice sports coat. Whether you are male or female, you will want to wear comfortable clothes and shoes. You need to be able to run with your dog and you certainly don't want to take a chance of falling and hurting yourself. Heaven forbid, if nothing else, you'll upset your dog. Women usually wear a dress or two-piece outfit, preferably with pockets to carry bait, comb, brush, etc. In this case men are the lucky ones with all their pockets. Ladies, think about where your dress will be if you need to kneel on the floor and also think about running. Does it allow freedom to do so?

You need to take along dog; crate; ex pen (if you use one); extra newspaper; water pail and water; all required grooming equipment, including hair dryer and extension cord; table; chair for you; bait for dog and lunch for you and friends; and, last but not least, clean up materials, such as plastic bags, paper towels, and perhaps a bath towel and some shampoo—just in case. Don't forget your entry confirmation and directions to the show.

If you are showing in obedience, then you will want to wear pants. Many of our top obedience handlers wear pants that are color-coordinated with their dogs. The philosophy is that imperfections in the black dog will be less obvious next to your black pants.

Whether you are showing in conformation, Junior Showmanship or obedience, you need to watch the clock and be sure you are not late. It is customary to pick up your conformation armband a few minutes before the start of the class. They will not wait for you and if you are on the show grounds and not in the ring, you will upset everyone. It's a little more complicated picking up your obedience armband if you show later in the class. If you have not picked up your armband and they get to your number, you may not be allowed to show. It's best to pick up your armband early, but then you may show earlier than expected if other handlers don't pick up. Customarily all conflicts should be discussed with the judge prior to the start of the class.

An exercise pen is one of the items you need to bring with you to a dog show, along with a water pail, grooming equipment, extra newspaper, lunch, and more.

Ch. Redthea Daniel of Rattlebridge, owned by Albert Snyder, Lamont Yoder, Meredith Johnson-Snyder and Anne Thaeder.

Junior Showmanship

The Junior Showmanship Class is a wonderful way to build self confidence even if there are no aspirations of staying with the dog-show game later in life. Frequently, Junior Showmanship becomes the background of those who become successful exhibitors/handlers in the future. In some instances it is taken very seriously, and success is measured in terms of wins. The Junior Handler is judged solely on his ability and skill in presenting his dog. The dog's conformation is not to be considered by the judge. Even so the condition and grooming of the dog may be a reflection upon the handler.

Usually the matches and point shows include different classes. The Junior Handler's dog may be entered in a breed or obedience class and even shown by another person in that class. Junior Showmanship classes are usually divided by age and perhaps sex. The age is determined by the handler's age on the day of the show.

CANINE GOOD CITIZEN

The AKC sponsors a program to encourage dog owners to train their dogs. Local clubs perform the pass/fail tests, and dogs who pass are awarded a Canine Good Citizen Certificate. Proof of vaccination is required at the time of participation. The test includes:

1. Accepting a friendly stranger.
2. Sitting politely for petting.
3. Appearance and grooming.
4. Walking on a loose leash.
5. Walking through a crowd.
6. Sit and down on command/staying in place.
7. Come when called.
8. Reaction to another dog.
9. Reactions to distractions.
10. Supervised separation.

If more effort was made by pet owners to accomplish these exercises, fewer dogs would be cast off to the humane shelter.

OBEDIENCE

Obedience is necessary, without a doubt, but it can also become a wonderful hobby or even an obsession. Obedience classes and competition can provide wonderful companionship, not only with

A canine good citizen must be able to get along with anyone, including other pets. This Cavalier has certainly passed the test!

your dog but with your classmates or fellow competitors. It is always gratifying to discuss your dog's problems with others who have had similar experiences. The AKC acknowledged obedience around 1936, and it has changed tremendously even though many of the exercises

All Cavaliers can benefit from obedience training to help them become wonderful house pets and companions.

are basically the same. Today, obedience competition is just that—very competitive. Even so, it is possible for every obedience exhibitor to come home a winner (by earning qualifying scores) even though he/she may not earn a placement in the class.

Most of the obedience titles are awarded after earning three qualifying scores (legs) in the appropriate class under three different judges. These classes offer a perfect score of 200, which is extremely rare. Each of the class exercises has its own point value. A leg is earned after receiving a score of at least 170 and at least 50 percent of the points available in each exercise. The titles are:

Companion Dog—CD
Companion Dog Excellent—CDX
Utility Dog—UD

After achieving the UD title, you may feel inclined to go after the UDX and/or OTCh. The UDX (Utility Dog Excellent) title went into effect in January 1994. It is not easily attained. The title requires qualifying simultaneously ten times in Open B and Utility B but not necessarily at consecutive shows.

The OTCh (Obedience Trial Champion) is awarded after the dog has earned his UD and then goes on to earn 100 championship points, a first place in Utility, a first place in Open and another first place in either class. The placements must be won under three different judges at all-breed obedience trials. The points are determined by the number of dogs competing in the Open B and Utility B classes. The OTCh title precedes the dog's name.

Obedience matches (AKC Sanctioned, Fun, and Show and Go) are usually available. Usually they are sponsored by the local obedience clubs. When preparing an obedience dog for a title, you will find matches very helpful. Fun Matches and Show and Go Matches are more lenient in allowing you to make corrections in the ring. This type of training is usually very necessary for the Open and Utility Classes. AKC Sanctioned Obedience Matches do not allow corrections in the ring since they must abide by the AKC Obedience Regulations. If you are interested in showing in obedience, then you should contact the AKC for a copy of the Obedience Regulations.

TRACKING

Tracking is officially classified obedience. There are three tracking titles available: Tracking Dog (TD), Tracking Dog Excellent (TDX), Variable Surface Tracking (VST). If all three tracking titles are obtained, then the dog officially becomes a CT (Champion Tracker). The CT will go in front of the dog's name.

A TD may be earned anytime and does not have to follow the other obedience titles. There are many exhibitors that prefer tracking to obedience, and there are others who do both.

AGILITY

Agility was first introduced by John Varley in England at the Crufts Dog Show, February 1978, but Peter Meanwell, competitor and judge, actually developed the idea. It was officially recognized in the early '80s. Agility is extremely popular in England and

What a natural! Lymrey Sweet Tart strikes a perfect show pose.

112

The versatile Cavalier King Charles Spaniel can do almost anything! This Cavalier has been trained as a therapy dog.

Canada and growing in popularity in the U.S. The AKC acknowledged agility in August 1994. Dogs must be at least 12 months of age to be entered. It is a fascinating sport that the dog, handler and spectators enjoy to the utmost. Agility is a spectator sport! The dog performs off lead. The handler either runs with his dog or positions himself on the course and directs his dog with verbal and hand signals over a timed course over or through a variety of obstacles including a time out or pause. One of the main drawbacks to agility is finding a place to train. The obstacles take up a lot of space and it is very time consuming to put up and take down courses.

The titles earned at AKC agility trials are Novice Agility Dog (NAD), Open Agility Dog (OAD), Agility Dog Excellent (ADX), and Master Agility Excellent (MAX). In order to acquire an agility title, a dog must earn a qualifying score in its respective class on three separate occasions under two different judges. The MAX will be awarded after earning ten qualifying scores in the Agility Excellent Class.

PERFORMANCE TESTS

During the last decade the American Kennel Club has promoted performance tests—those events that test the different breeds' natural abilities. This type of event encourages a handler to devote even more time to his dog and retain the natural instincts of his breed heritage. It is an important part of the wonderful world of dogs.

Hunting Titles

For retrievers, pointing breeds and spaniels. Titles offered are Junior Hunter (JH), Senior Hunter (SH), and Master Hunter (MH).

Flushing Spaniels Their primary purpose is to hunt, find, flush and return birds to hand as quickly as possible in a pleasing and obedient manner. The entrant must be at least six months of age and dogs with limited registration (ILP) are eligible. Game used are pigeons, pheasants, and quail.

Retrievers Limited registration (ILP) retrievers are not eligible to compete in Hunting Tests. The purpose of a Hunting Test for retrievers is to test the merits of and evaluate the abilities of retrievers in the field in order to determine their suitability and ability as hunting companions. They are expected to retrieve any type of game bird, pheasants, ducks, pigeons, guinea hens and quail.

Pointing Breeds Are eligible at six months of age, and dogs with limited registration (ILP) are permitted. They must show a keen desire to hunt; be bold and independent; have a fast, yet attractive, manner of hunting; and demonstrate intelligence not only in seeking objectives but also in the ability to find game. They must establish point, and in the more advanced tests they need to be steady to wing and must remain in position until the bird is shot or they are released.

A Senior Hunter must retrieve. A Master Hunter must honor. The judges and the marshal are permitted to ride horseback during the test, but all handling must be done on foot.

GENERAL INFORMATION

Obedience, tracking and agility allow the purebred dog with an Indefinite Listing Privilege (ILP) number or a limited registration

It is an inherent trait of the Cavalier breed to use their sense of smell and ability to track and flush out wild game—maybe one of these pups will grow to be a title winner.

to be exhibited and earn titles. Application must be made to the AKC for an ILP number.

The American Kennel Club publishes a monthly *Events* magazine that is part of the *Gazette*, their official journal for the sport of purebred dogs. The *Events* section lists upcoming shows and the secretary or superintendent for them. The majority of the conformation shows in the U.S. are overseen by licensed superintendents. Generally the entry closing date is approximately two-and-a-half weeks before the actual show. Point shows are fairly expensive, while the match shows cost about one third of the point show entry fee. Match shows usually take entries the day of the show but some are pre-entry. The best way to find match show information is through your local kennel club. Upon asking, the AKC can provide you with a list of superintendents, and you can write and ask to be put on their mailing lists.

Obedience trial and tracking test information is available through the AKC. Frequently these events are not superintended, but put on by the host club. Therefore you would make the entry with the event's secretary.

As you have read, there are numerous activities you can share with your dog. Regardless what you do, it does take teamwork. Your dog can only benefit from your attention and training. We hope this chapter has enlightened you and hope, if nothing else, you will attend a show here and there. Perhaps you will start with a puppy kindergarten class, and who knows where it may lead!

HEALTH CARE

Veterinary medicine has become far more sophisticated than what was available to our ancestors. This can be attributed to the increase in household pets and consequently the demand for better care for them. Also human medicine has become far more complex. Today diagnostic testing in veterinary medicine parallels human diagnostics. Because of better technology we can expect our pets to live healthier lives thereby increasing their life spans.

THE FIRST CHECK UP

You will want to take your new puppy/dog in for its first check up within 48 to 72 hours after acquiring it. Many breeders strongly recommend this check up and so do the humane shelters. A puppy/dog can appear healthy but it may have a serious problem that is not apparent to the layman. Most pets have some type of a minor flaw that may never cause a real problem.

Unfortunately if he/she should have a serious problem, you will want to consider the consequences of keeping the pet and the attachments that will be formed, which may be broken prematurely. Keep in mind there are many healthy dogs looking for good homes.

This first check up is a good time to establish yourself with the veterinarian and learn the office policy regarding their hours and how they handle emergencies. Usually the breeder or another conscientious pet owner is a good reference for locating a capable veterinarian. You should be aware that not all veterinarians give the same quality of service. Please do not make your selection on the least expensive clinic, as they may be short changing your pet. There is the possibility that eventually it will cost you more due to improper diagnosis, treatment, etc. If you are selecting a new veterinarian, feel free to ask for a tour of the clinic. You should inquire about making an appointment for a tour since all clinics are working clinics, and therefore may not be available all day for sightseers. You may worry less if you see where your pet will be spending the day if he ever needs to be hospitalized.

THE PHYSICAL EXAM

Your veterinarian will check your pet's overall condition, which

It is never too early to begin health care for your Cavalier puppy. In fact, it is imperative that you bring him to a veterinarian within the first 48-72 hours after acquiring him.

includes listening to the heart; checking the respiration; feeling the abdomen, muscles and joints; checking the mouth, which includes the gum color and signs of gum disease along with plaque buildup; checking the ears for signs of an infection or ear mites; examining the eyes; and, last but not least, checking the condition of the skin and coat.

He should ask you questions regarding your pet's eating and elimination habits and invite you to relay your questions. It is a good idea to prepare a list so as not to forget anything. He should discuss the proper diet and the quantity to be fed. If this should differ from your breeder's recommendation, then you should convey to him the breeder's choice and see if he approves. If he recommends changing the diet, then this should be done over a few days so as not to cause a gastrointestinal upset. It is customary to take in a fresh stool sample (just a small amount) for a test for intestinal parasites. It must be fresh, preferably within 12 hours, since the eggs hatch quickly and after hatching will not be observed under the microscope. If your pet isn't obliging then, usually the technician can take one in the clinic.

Have a discussion with the veterinarian about the proper diet and feeding schedule for your new Cavalier puppy.

IMMUNIZATIONS

It is important that you take your puppy/dog's vaccination record with you on your first visit. In case of a puppy, presumably the breeder has seen to the vaccinations up to the time you acquired custody. Veterinarians differ in their vaccination protocol. It is not unusual for your puppy to have received vaccinations for distemper, hepatitis, leptospirosis, parvovirus, corona virus, and parainfluenza every two to three weeks from the age

Puppies are immune to disease from their mother while they are nursing. After that, your veterinarian will recommend certain immunizations at the right age for your pup.

of five or six weeks. Usually this is a combined injection and is typically called the DHLPP. The DHLPP is given through at least 12 to 14 weeks of age, and it is customary to continue with another parvovirus vaccine at 16 to 18 weeks. You may wonder why so many immunizations are necessary. No one knows for sure when the puppy's maternal antibodies are gone, although it is customarily accepted that distemper antibodies are gone by 12 weeks. Usually parvovirus antibodies are gone by 16 to 18 weeks of age. However, it is possible for the maternal antibodies to be gone at a much earlier age or even a later age. Therefore immunizations are started at an early age. The vaccine will not give immunity as long as there are maternal antibodies.

The rabies vaccination is given at three or six months of age depending on your local laws. A vaccine for bordetella (kennel cough) is advisable and can be given anytime from the age of five weeks. The coronavirus is not commonly given unless there is a problem locally. The Lyme vaccine is necessary in endemic areas. Lyme disease has been reported in 47 states.

Distemper

This is virtually an incurable disease. If the dog recovers, he is subject to severe nervous disorders. The virus attacks every tissue in the body and resembles a bad cold with a fever. It can cause a runny nose and eyes and cause gastrointestinal disorders, including a poor appetite, vomiting and diarrhea. The virus is carried by raccoons, foxes, wolves, mink and other dogs. Unvaccinated youngsters and senior citizens are very susceptible. This is still a common disease.

Hepatitis

This is a virus that is most serious in very young dogs. It is spread by contact with an infected animal or its stool or urine. The virus affects the liver and kidneys and is characterized by high fever, depression and lack of appetite. Recovered animals may be afflicted with chronic illnesses.

Leptospirosis

This is a bacterial disease transmitted by contact with the urine of an infected dog, rat or other wildlife. It produces severe symptoms of fever, depression, jaundice and internal bleeding and was fatal before the vaccine was developed. Recovered dogs can be carriers, and the disease can be transmitted from dogs to humans.

Parvovirus

This was first noted in the late 1970s and is still a fatal disease. However, with proper vaccinations, early diagnosis and prompt

A reputable boarding kennel will require that dogs receive the vaccination for kennel cough no less than two weeks before their scheduled stay.

Puppies are vulnerable to many diseases, which is why immunizations are so vital.

treatment, it is a manageable disease. It attacks the bone marrow and intestinal tract. The symptoms include depression, loss of appetite, vomiting, diarrhea and collapse. Immediate medical attention is of the essence.

Rabies

This is shed in the saliva and is carried by raccoons, skunks, foxes, other dogs and cats. It attacks nerve tissue, resulting in paralysis and death. Rabies can be transmitted to people and is virtually always fatal. This disease is reappearing in the suburbs.

Bordetella (Kennel Cough)

The symptoms are coughing, sneezing, hacking and retching accompanied by nasal discharge usually lasting from a few days to several weeks. There are several disease-producing organisms responsible for this disease. The present vaccines are helpful but do

Bordatella attached to canine cilia. Otherwise known as kennel cough, this disease is highly contagious and should be vaccinated against routinely.

not protect for all the strains. It usually is not life threatening but in some instances it can progress to a serious bronchopneumonia. The disease is highly contagious. The vaccination should be given routinely for dogs that come in contact with other dogs, such as through boarding, training class or visits to the groomer.

Coronavirus

This is usually self limiting and not life threatening. It was first noted in the late '70s about a year before parvovirus. The virus produces a yellow/brown stool and there may be depression, vomiting and diarrhea.

Lyme Disease

This was first diagnosed in the United States in 1976 in Lyme, CT in people who lived in close proximity to the deer tick. Symptoms may include acute lameness, fever, swelling of

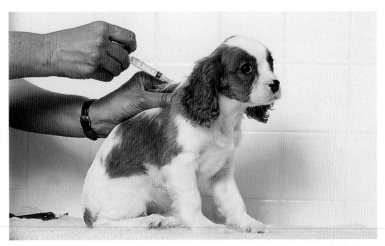

Your veterinarian will put your Cavalier puppy on an immunization schedule.

joints and loss of appetite. Your veterinarian can advise you if you live in an endemic area.

After your puppy has completed his puppy vaccinations, you will continue to booster the DHLPP once a year. It is customary to booster the rabies one year after the first vaccine and then, depending on where you live, it should be boostered every year or every three years. This depends on your local laws. The Lyme and corona vaccines are boostered annually and it is recommended that the bordetella be boostered every six to eight months.

The deer tick is the most common carrier of Lyme disease. Photo courtesy of Virbac Laboratories, Fort Worth, Texas.

ANNUAL VISIT

I would like to impress the importance of the annual check up, which would include the booster vaccinations, check for intestinal parasites and test for heartworm. Today in our very busy world it is rush, rush and see "how much you can get for how little." Unbelievably, some non-veterinary businesses have entered into the vaccination business. More harm than good can come to your dog through improper vaccinations, possibly from inferior vaccines and/or the wrong schedule. More than likely you truly care about your companion dog and over the years you have devoted much time and expense to his well being. Perhaps you are unaware that a vaccination is not just a vaccination. There is more involved. Please, please follow through with regular physical examinations. It is so important for your veterinarian to know your dog and this is especially true during middle age through the geriatric years. More than likely your older dog will require more than one physical a year. The annual physical is good preventive medicine. Through early diagnosis and subsequent treatment your dog can maintain a longer and better quality of life.

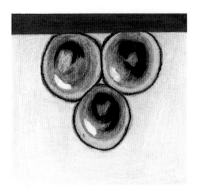

Roundworm eggs, as seen on a fecal evaluation. The eggs must develop for at least 12 days before they are infectious.

INTESTINAL PARASITES

Hookworms

These are almost microscopic intestinal worms that can cause anemia and therefore serious problems, including death, in young puppies. Hookworms can be transmitted to humans through penetration of the skin. Puppies may be born with them.

Roundworms

These are spaghetti-like worms that can cause a potbellied appearance and dull coat along with more severe symptoms, such as vomiting, diarrhea and coughing. Puppies acquire these while in the mother's uterus and through lactation. Both hookworms and roundworms may be acquired through ingestion.

Whipworms

These have a three-month life cycle and are not acquired through the dam. They cause intermittent diarrhea usually with mucus. Whipworms are possibly the most difficult worm to eradicate. Their eggs are very resistant to most environmental factors and can last for years until the proper conditions enable them to mature. Whipworms are seldom seen in the stool.

Intestinal parasites are more prevalent in some areas than others. Climate, soil and contamination are big factors contributing to the incidence of intestinal parasites. Eggs are passed in the stool, lay on the ground and then become infective in a certain number of days. Each of the above worms has a different life cycle. Your best chance of becoming and remaining worm-free is to always pooper-scoop your yard. A fenced-in yard keeps stray dogs out, which is certainly helpful.

I would recommend having a fecal examination on your dog twice a year or more often if there is a problem. If your dog has a positive fecal sample, then he will be given the appropriate medication and you will be asked to bring back another stool sample in a certain period of time (depending on the type of worm) and then be rewormed. This process goes on until he has at least two negative samples. The different types of worms require different medications. You will be wasting your money and doing your dog an injustice by buying over-the-counter medication without first consulting your veterinarian.

OTHER INTERNAL PARASITES

Coccidiosis and Giardiasis

These protozoal infections usually affect puppies, especially in places where large numbers of puppies are brought together. Older dogs may harbor these infections but

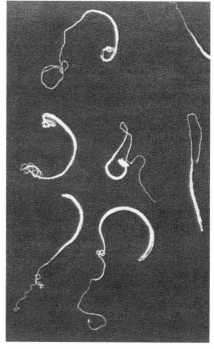

Whipworms are difficult to find and it is a job best left to a veterinarian. Pictured here are adult whipworms.

do not show signs unless they are stressed. Symptoms include diarrhea, weight loss and lack of appetite. These infections are not always apparent in the fecal examination.

Tapeworms

Seldom apparent on fecal floatation, they are diagnosed frequently as rice-like segments around the dog's anus and the base of the tail. Tapeworms are long, flat and ribbon like, sometimes several feet in length, and made up of many segments about five-eighths of an inch long. The two most common types of tapeworms found in the dog are:
(1) First the larval form of the flea tapeworm parasite must mature in an intermediate host, the flea, before it can become infective. Your dog acquires this by ingesting the flea through licking and chewing.

(2) Rabbits, rodents and certain large game animals serve as intermediate hosts for other species of tapeworms. If your dog should eat one of these infected hosts, then he can acquire tapeworms.

Heartworm Disease

This is a worm that resides in the heart and adjacent blood vessels of the lung that produces microfilaria, which circulate in the bloodstream. It is possible for a dog to be infected with any number of worms from one to a hundred that can be 6 to 14 inches long. It is a life-threatening disease, expensive to treat and easily prevented. Depending on where you live, your veterinarian may recommend a preventive year-round and either an annual or semiannual blood test. The most common preventive is given once a month.

A healthy Cavalier King Charles Spaniel will be able to participate in all kinds of activities.

External Parasites

Fleas

These pests are not only the dog's worst enemy but also enemy to the owner's pocketbook. Preventing is less expensive than treating, but regardless we'd prefer to spend our money elsewhere. Likely, the majority of our dogs are allergic to the bite of a flea, and in many cases it only takes one flea bite. The protein in the flea's saliva is the culprit. Allergic dogs have a reaction, which usually results in a "hot spot." More

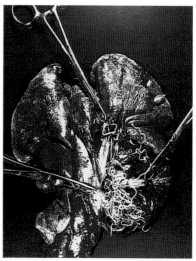

Dirofilaria—adult heart worms in the heart of a dog. Courtesy of Merck Ag Vet.

than likely such a reaction will involve a trip to the veterinarian for treatment. Yes, prevention is less expensive. Fortunately today there are several good products available.

If there is a flea infestation, no one product is going to correct the problem. Not only will the dog require treatment so will the environment. In general flea collars are not very effective although there is now available an "egg" collar that will kill the eggs on the dog. Dips are the most economical but they are messy. There are some effective shampoos and treatments available through pet shops and veterinarians. An oral tablet arrived on the American market in 1995 and was popular in Europe the previous year. It sterilizes the female flea but will not kill adult fleas. Therefore the tablet, which is given monthly, will decrease the flea population but is not a "cure-all." Those dogs that suffer from flea-bite allergy will still be subjected to the bite of the flea. Another popular parasiticide is permethrin, which is applied to the back of the dog in one or two places depending on the dog's weight. This product works as a repellent causing the flea to get "hot feet" and jump off. Do not confuse this product with some of the organophosphates that are also applied to the dog's back.

Some products are not usable on young puppies. Treating fleas should be done under your veterinarian's guidance. Frequently it is necessary to combine products and the layman does not have the knowledge regarding possible toxicities. It is hard to believe but there are a few dogs that do have a natural resistance to fleas. Nevertheless it would be wise to treat all pets at the same time. Don't forget your cats. Cats just love to prowl the neighborhood and consequently return with unwanted guests.

Adult fleas live on the dog but their eggs drop off the dog into the environment. There they go through four larval stages before reaching adulthood, and thereby are able to jump back on the poor unsuspecting dog. The cycle resumes and takes between 21 to 28 days under ideal conditions. There are environmental products available that will kill both the adult fleas and the larvae.

Ticks

Ticks carry Rocky Mountain Spotted Fever, Lyme disease and can cause tick paralysis. They should be removed with tweezers, trying to pull out the head. The jaws carry disease. There is a tick preventive collar that does an excellent job. The ticks automatically back out on those dogs wearing collars.

Sarcoptic Mange

This is a mite that is difficult to find on skin scrapings. The pinnal reflex is a good indicator of this disease. Rub the ends of the pinna (ear) together and the dog will start scratching with his foot. Sarcoptes are highly contagious to other dogs and to humans although they do not live long on humans. They cause intense itching.

Demodectic Mange

This is a mite that is passed from the dam to her puppies. It affects youngsters age three to ten months. Diagnosis is confirmed by skin scraping. Small areas of alopecia around the eyes, lips and/or forelegs become visible. There is little itching unless there is a secondary bacterial infection. Some breeds are afflicted more than others.

Cheyletiella

This causes intense itching and is diagnosed by skin scraping. It lives in the outer layers of the skin of dogs, cats, rabbits and humans. Yellow-gray scales may be found on the back and the rump, top of the head and the nose.

To Breed or Not To Breed

More than likely your breeder has requested that you have your puppy neutered or spayed. Your breeder's request is based on what is healthiest for your dog and what is most beneficial for your breed. Experienced and conscientious breeders devote many years into developing a bloodline. In order to do this, he makes every effort to plan each breeding in regard to conformation, temperament and health. This type of breeder does his best to perform the necessary testing (i.e., OFA, CERF, testing for inherited blood disorders, thyroid, etc.). Testing is expensive and sometimes very disheartening when a favorite dog doesn't pass his health tests. The health history pertains not only to the breeding stock but to the immediate ancestors. Reputable breeders do not want their offspring to be bred indiscriminately. Therefore you may be asked to neuter or spay

Check your Cavalier's coat carefully for parasites, especially after he has been playing outside.

Reputable breeders will request that you have your Cavalier spayed or neutered to ensure a healthy dog and to avoid indiscriminate breeding.

your puppy. Of course there is always the exception, and your breeder may agree to let you breed your dog under his direct supervision. This is an important concept. More and more effort is being made to breed healthier dogs.

Spay/Neuter

There are numerous benefits of performing this surgery at six months of age. Unspayed females are subject to mammary and ovarian cancer. In order to prevent mammary cancer she must be spayed prior to her first heat cycle. Later in life, an unspayed female may develop a pyometra (an infected uterus), which is definitely life threatening.

Spaying is performed under a general anesthetic and is easy on the young dog. As you might expect it is a little harder on the older dog, but that is no reason to deny her the surgery. The surgery removes the ovaries and uterus. It is important to remove all the ovarian tissue. If some is left behind, she could remain attractive to males. In order to view the ovaries, a reasonably long incision is necessary. An ovariohysterectomy is considered major surgery.

Neutering the male at a young age will inhibit some characteristic male behavior that owners frown upon. Some boys will not hike their legs and mark territory if they are neutered at six months of age. Also neutering at a young age has hormonal benefits, lessening the chance of hormonal aggressiveness.

Surgery involves removing the testicles but leaving the scrotum. If there should be a retained testicle, then he definitely needs to be neutered before the age of two or three years. Retained testicles can develop into cancer. Unneutered males are at risk for testicular cancer, perineal fistulas, perianal tumors and fistulas and prostatic disease.

Intact males and females are prone to housebreaking accidents. Females urinate frequently before, during and after heat cycles, and males tend to mark territory if there is a female in heat. Males may show the same behavior if there is a visiting dog or guests.

Surgery involves a sterile operating procedure equivalent to human surgery. The incision site is shaved, surgically scrubbed and draped. The veterinarian wears a sterile surgical gown, cap, mask and gloves. Anesthesia should be monitored by a registered technician. It is customary for the veterinarian to recommend a pre-anesthetic blood screening, looking for metabolic problems and a ECG rhythm strip to check for normal heart function. Today anesthetics are equal to human anesthetics, which enables your dog to walk out of the clinic the same day as surgery.

Some folks worry about their dog gaining weight after being neutered or spayed. This is usually not the case. It is true that some dogs may be less active so they could develop a problem, but most dogs are just as active as they were before surgery. However, if your dog should begin to gain, then you need to decrease his food and see to it that he gets a little more exercise.

BEHAVIOR and Canine Communication

Studies of the human/animal bond point out the importance of the unique relationships that exist between people and their pets. Those of us who share our lives with pets understand the special part they play through companionship, service and protection. For many, the pet/owner bond goes beyond simple companionship; pets are often considered members of the family. A leading pet food manufacturer recently conducted a nationwide survey of pet owners to gauge just how important pets were in their lives. Here's what they found:

- 76 percent allow their pets to sleep on their beds
- 78 percent think of their pets as their children
- 84 percent display photos of their pets, mostly in their homes
- 84 percent think that their pets react to their own emotions
- 100 percent talk to their pets
- 97 percent think that their pets understand what they're saying
Are you surprised?

Senior citizens show more concern for their own eating habits when they have the responsibility of feeding a dog. Seeing that their dog is routinely exercised encourages the owner to think of schedules that otherwise may seem unimportant to the senior citizen. The older owner may be arthritic and feeling poorly but with responsibility for his dog he has a reason to get up and get moving. It is a big plus if his dog is an attention seeker who will demand such from his owner.

Over the last couple of decades, it has been shown that pets relieve the stress of those who lead busy lives. Owning a pet has been known to lessen the occurrence of heart attack and stroke.

Many single folks thrive on the companionship of a dog. Lifestyles are very different from a long time ago, and today more individuals seek the single life. However, they receive fulfillment from owning a dog.

Most likely the majority of our dogs live in family environments. The companionship they provide is well worth the effort involved. In my opinion, every child should have the opportunity to have a family dog. Dogs teach responsibility through understanding their care, feelings and even respecting their life cycles. Frequently those children who have not been exposed to dogs grow up afraid of dogs, which isn't good. Dogs sense timidity and some will take advantage of the situation.

Today more dogs are serving as service dogs. Since the origination of the Seeing Eye dogs years ago, we now have trained hearing dogs. Also dogs are trained to provide service for the handicapped and are able to perform many different tasks for their owners. Search and Rescue dogs, with their handlers, are sent throughout the world to assist in recovery of disaster victims. They are life savers.

The presence of a dog in the family teaches children a sense of responsibility and gives them a fun companion and playmate.

Therapy dogs are very popular with nursing homes, and some hospitals even allow them to visit. The inhabitants truly look forward to their visits. They wanted and were allowed to have visiting dogs in their beds to hold and love.

Nationally there is a Pet Awareness Week to educate students and others about the value and basic care of our pets. Many countries take an even greater interest in their pets than Americans do. In those countries the pets are allowed to accompany their owners into restaurants and shops, etc. In the U.S. this freedom is only available to our service dogs. Even so we think very highly of the human/animal bond.

CANINE BEHAVIOR

Canine behavior problems are the number-one reason for pet owners to dispose of their dogs, either through new homes, humane shelters or euthanasia. Unfortunately there are too many owners who are unwilling to devote the necessary time to properly train their dogs. On the other hand, there are those who not only are concerned about inherited health problems but are also aware of the dog's mental stability.

You may realize that a breed and his group relatives (i.e., sporting, hounds, etc.) show tendencies to behavioral characteristics.

An experienced breeder can acquaint you with his breed's personality. Unfortunately many breeds are labeled with poor temperaments when actually the breed as a whole is not affected but only a small percentage of individuals within the breed.

Inheritance and environment contribute to the dog's behavior. Some naïve people suggest inbreeding as the cause of bad temperaments. Inbreeding only results in poor behavior if the ancestors carry the trait. If there are excellent temperaments behind the dogs, then inbreeding will promote good temperaments in the offspring. Did you ever consider that inbreeding is what sets the characteristics of a breed? A purebred dog is the end result of inbreeding. This does not spare the mixed-breed dog from the same problems. Mixed-breed dogs frequently are the offspring of purebred dogs.

Not too many decades ago most of our dogs led a different lifestyle than what is prevalent today. Usually mom stayed home so the dog had human companionship and someone to discipline it if needed. Not much was expected from the dog. Today's mom works and everyone's life is at a much faster pace.

The dog may have to adjust to being a "weekend" dog. The family is gone all day during the week, and the dog is left to his own devices for entertainment. Some dogs sleep all day waiting for their family to come home and others become wigwam wreckers if given

Socialization with littermates is very important to the development of your Cavalier's personality.

the opportunity. Crates do ensure the safety of the dog and the house. However, he could become a physically and emotionally cripple if he doesn't get enough exercise and attention. We still appreciate and want the companionship of our dogs although we expect more from them. In many cases we tend to forget dogs are just that—*dogs* not human beings.

Cavaliers will need plenty of your time, care, and attention in order to thrive and lead a quality life.

SOCIALIZING AND TRAINING

Many prospective puppy buyers lack experience regarding the proper socialization and training needed to develop the type of pet we all desire. In the first 18 months, training does take some work. It is easier to start proper training before there is a problem that needs to be corrected.

The initial work begins with the breeder. The breeder should start socializing the puppy at five to six weeks of age and cannot let up. Human socializing is critical up through 12 weeks of age and likewise important during the following months. The litter should be left together during the first few weeks but it is necessary to separate them by ten weeks of age. Leaving them together after that time will increase competition for litter dominance. If puppies are not socialized with people by 12 weeks of age, they may be timid in later life.

The eight- to ten-week age period is a fearful time for puppies. They need to be handled very gently around children and adults. There should be no harsh discipline during this time. Starting at 14 weeks of age, the puppy begins the juvenile period, which ends when he reaches sexual maturity around six to 14 months of age. During the juvenile period he needs to be introduced to strangers (adults, children and other dogs) on the home property. At sexual maturity he will begin to bark at strangers and become more protective. Males start to lift their legs to urinate but if you desire you can inhibit this behavior by walking your boy on leash away from trees, shrubs, fences, etc.

Perhaps you are thinking about an older puppy. You need to inquire about the puppy's social experience. If he has lived without socialization, he may have a hard time adjusting to people and environmental stimuli. Assuming he has had a good social upbringing, there are advantages to an older puppy.

Training includes puppy kindergarten and a minimum of one to two basic training classes. During these classes you will learn how to dominate your youngster. This is especially important if you own a large breed of dog. It is somewhat harder, if not nearly impossible, for some owners to be the Alpha figure when their dog towers over them. You will be taught how to properly restrain your dog. This concept is important. Again it puts you in the Alpha position. All dogs need to be restrained many times during their lives. Believe it or not, some of our worst offenders are the eight-week-old puppies that are brought to our clinic. They need to be gently restrained for a nail trim but the way they carry on you would think we were killing them. In comparison, their vaccination is a "piece of cake." When we ask dogs to do something that is not agreeable to them, then their worst comes out. Life will be easier for your dog if you expose him at a young age to the necessities of life—proper behavior and restraint.

UNDERSTANDING THE DOG'S LANGUAGE

Most authorities agree that the dog is a descendent of the wolf. The dog and wolf have similar traits. For instance both are pack

When socializing your young Cavalier, puppy kindergarten can really make a playful extrovert out of him and help him to make many friends.

oriented and prefer not to be isolated for long periods of time. Another characteristic is that the dog, like the wolf, looks to the leader—Alpha—for direction. Both the wolf and the dog communicate through body language, not only within their pack but with outsiders.

Every pack has an Alpha figure. The dog looks to you, or should look to you, to be that leader. If your dog doesn't receive the proper training and guidance, he very well may replace you as Alpha. This would be a serious problem and is certainly a disservice to your dog.

Dogs have a certain language, and it is up to the owner to try to understand what her Cavalier is telling her.

Eye contact is one way the Alpha wolf keeps order within his pack. You are Alpha so you must establish eye contact with your puppy. Obviously your puppy will have to look at you. Practice eye contact even if you need to hold his head for five to ten seconds at a time. You can give him a treat as a reward. Make sure your eye contact is gentle and not threatening. Later, if he has been naughty, it is permissible to give him a long, penetrating look. There are some older dogs that never learned eye contact as puppies and cannot accept eye contact. You should avoid eye contact with these dogs since they feel threatened and will retaliate as such.

BODY LANGUAGE

The play bow, when the forequarters are down and the hindquarters are elevated, is an invitation to play. Puppies play fight, which helps them learn the acceptable limits of biting. This is necessary for later in their lives. Nevertheless, an owner may be falsely reassured by the playful nature of his dog's aggression. Playful aggression toward another dog or human may be an indication of serious aggression in the future. Owners should never play fight or play tug-of-war with any dog that is inclined to be dominant.

Signs of submission are:

1. Avoids eye contact.
2. Active submission—the dog crouches down, ears back and the tail is lowered.
3. Passive submission—the dog rolls on his side with his hindlegs in the air and frequently urinates.

Signs of dominance are:

1. Makes eye contact.
2. Stands with ears up, tail up and the hair raised on his neck.
3. Shows dominance over another dog by standing at right angles over it.

Dominant dogs tend to behave in characteristic ways such as:

1. The dog may be unwilling to move from his place (i.e., reluctant to give up the sofa if the owner wants to sit there).
2. He may not part with toys or objects in his mouth and may show possessiveness with his food bowl.
3. He may not respond quickly to commands.
4. He may be disagreeable for grooming and dislikes to be petted.

Dogs are popular because of their sociable nature. Those that have contact with humans during the first 12 weeks of life regard them as a member of their own species—their pack. All dogs have the potential for both dominant and submissive behavior. Only through experience and training do they learn to whom it is appropriate to show which behavior. Not all dogs are concerned with dominance but owners need to be aware of that potential. It is wise for the owner to establish his dominance early on.

A human can express dominance or submission toward a dog in the following ways:

1. Meeting the dog's gaze signals dominance. Averting the gaze signals submission. If the dog growls or threatens, averting the gaze is the first avoiding action to take—it may prevent attack. It is important to establish eye contact in the puppy. The older dog that has not been exposed to eye contact may see it as a threat and will not be willing to submit.
2. Being taller than the dog signals dominance; being lower signals submission. This is why, when attempting to make friends

with a strange dog or catch the runaway, one should kneel down to his level. Some owners see their dogs become dominant when allowed on the furniture or on the bed. Then he is at the owner's level.

3. An owner can gain dominance by ignoring all the dog's social initiatives. The owner pays attention to the dog only when he obeys a command.

No dog should be allowed to achieve dominant status over any adult or child. Ways of preventing are as follows:

1. Handle the puppy gently, especially during the three- to four-month period.

2. Let the children and adults handfeed him and teach him to take food without lunging or grabbing.

3. Do not allow him to chase children or joggers.

4. Do not allow him to jump on people or mount their legs. Even females may be inclined to mount. It is not only a male habit.

5. Do not allow him to growl for any reason.

6. Don't participate in wrestling or tug-of-war games.

7. Don't physically punish puppies for aggressive behavior.

You should be able to tell a puppy's temperament by watching him play with his littermates.

Restrain him from repeating the infraction and teach an alternative behavior. Dogs should earn everything they receive from their owners. This would include sitting to receive petting or treats, sitting before going out the door and sitting to receive the collar and leash. These types of exercises reinforce the owner's dominance.

Young children should never be left alone with a dog. It is important that children learn some basic obedience commands so they have some control over the dog. They will gain the respect of their dog.

FEAR

One of the most common problems dogs experience is being fearful. Some dogs are more afraid than others. On the lesser side, which is sometimes humorous to watch, dogs can be afraid of a strange object. They act silly when something is out of place in the house. We call his problem perceptive intelligence. He realizes the abnormal within his known environment. He does not react the same way in strange environments since he does not know what is normal.

On the more serious side is a fear of people. This can result in backing off, seeking his own space and saying "leave me alone" or it can result in an aggressive behavior that may lead to challenging the person. Respect that the dog wants to be left alone and give him time to come forward. If you approach the cornered dog, he may resort to snapping. If you leave him alone, he may decide to come forward, which should be rewarded with a treat.

Some dogs may initially be too fearful to take treats. In these cases it is helpful to make sure the dog hasn't eaten for about 24 hours. Being a little hungry encourages him to accept the treats, especially if they are of the "gourmet" variety.

Dogs can be afraid of numerous things, including loud noises and thunderstorms. Invariably the owner rewards (by comforting) the dog when it shows signs of fearfulness. When your dog is frightened, direct his attention to something else and act happy. Don't dwell on his fright.

AGGRESSION

Some different types of aggression are: predatory, defensive, dominance, possessive, protective, fear induced, noise provoked,

Body language can tell you how your dog is feeling. This Cavalier's play bow indicates that he is ready for some fun.

"rage" syndrome (unprovoked aggression), maternal and aggression directed toward other dogs. Aggression is the most common behavioral problem encountered. Protective breeds are expected to be more aggressive than others but with the proper upbringing they can make very dependable companions. You need to be able to read your dog.

Many factors contribute to aggression including genetics and environment. An improper environment, which may include the living conditions, lack of social life, excessive punishment, being attacked or frightened by an aggressive dog, etc., can all influence a dog's behavior. Even spoiling him and giving too much praise may be detrimental. Isolation and the lack of human contact or exposure to frequent teasing by children or adults also can ruin a good dog.

Lack of direction, fear, or confusion lead to aggression in those dogs that are so inclined. Any obedience exercise, even the sit and down, can direct the dog and overcome fear and/or confusion. Every dog should learn these commands as a youngster, and there should be periodic reinforcement.

When a dog is showing signs of aggression, you should speak calmly (no screaming or hysterics) and firmly give a command that he understands, such as the sit. As soon as your dog obeys, you have assumed your dominant position. Aggression presents a problem because there may be danger to others. Sometimes it is an emotional issue. Owners may consciously or unconsciously encourage their dog's aggression. Other owners show responsibility by accepting the problem and taking measures to keep it under control. The owner is responsible

Socialization is very important for your Cavalier. The more people he meets, the better socialized he will become.

Take your Cavalier with you wherever you go and introduce him to as many people and situations as possible.

for his dog's actions, and it is not wise to take a chance on someone being bitten, especially a child. Euthanasia is the solution for some owners and in severe cases this may be the best choice. However, few dogs are that dangerous and very few are that much of a threat to their owners. If caution is exercised and professional help is gained early on, most cases can be controlled.

Some authorities recommend feeding a lower protein (less than 20 percent) diet. They believe this can aid in reducing aggression. If the dog loses weight, then vegetable oil can be added. Veterinarians and behaviorists are having some success with pharmacology. In many cases treatment is possible and can improve the situation.

If you have done everything according to "the book" regarding training and socializing and are still having a behavior problem, don't procrastinate. It is important that the problem gets attention before it is out of hand. It is estimated that 20 percent of a veterinarian's time may be devoted to dealing with problems before they become so intolerable that the dog is separated from its home and owner. If your veterinarian isn't able to help, he should refer you to a behaviorist.

DENTAL CARE for Your Dog's Life

So you've got a new puppy! You also have a new set of puppy teeth in your household. Anyone who has ever raised a puppy is abundantly aware of these new teeth. Your puppy will chew anything it can reach, chase your shoelaces, and play "tear the rag" with any piece of clothing it can find. When puppies are newly born, they have no teeth. At about four weeks of age, puppies of most breeds begin to develop their deciduous or baby teeth. They begin eating semi-solid food, fighting and biting with their litter mates, and learning discipline from their mother. As their new teeth come in, they inflict more pain on their mother's breasts, so her feeding sessions become less frequent and shorter. By six or eight weeks, the mother will start growling to warn her pups when they are fighting too roughly or hurting her as they nurse too much with their new teeth.

Puppies need to chew. It is a necessary part of their physical and mental development. They develop muscles and necessary life skills as they drag objects around, fight over possession, and vocalize alerts and warnings. Puppies chew on things to explore their world. They are using their sense of taste to determine what is food and what is not. How else can they tell an electrical cord from a lizard? At about four months of age, most puppies begin shedding their baby teeth. Often these teeth need some help to come out and make

A safe chew toy will keep your puppy from chewing on your belongings.

This Cavalier loves to spend time playing with his toys.

way for the permanent teeth. The incisors (front teeth) will be replaced first. Then, the adult canine or fang teeth erupt. When the baby tooth is not shed before the permanent tooth comes in, veterinarians call it a retained deciduous tooth. This condition will often cause gum infections by trapping hair and debris between the permanent tooth and the retained baby tooth. Nylafloss® is an excellent device for puppies to use. They can toss it, drag it, and chew on the many surfaces it presents. The baby teeth can catch in the nylon material, aiding in their removal. Puppies that have adequate chew toys will have less destructive behavior, develop more physically, and have less chance of retained deciduous teeth.

During the first year, your dog should be seen by your veterinarian at regular intervals. Your veterinarian will let you know when to bring in your puppy for vaccinations and parasite examinations. At each visit, your veterinarian should inspect the lips, teeth, and mouth as part of a complete physical examination. You should take some part in the maintenance of your dog's oral health. You should examine your dog's mouth weekly throughout his first year to make sure there are no sores, foreign objects, tooth problems, etc. If your dog drools excessively, shakes its head, or has bad breath, consult your veterinarian. By the time your dog is six months old, the permanent teeth are all in and plaque can start to accumulate on the tooth surfaces. This is when your dog needs to develop good dental-care habits to prevent calculus build-up on its teeth. Brushing is best. That is a fact that cannot be denied. However, some dogs do

Tooth decay is a dangerous problem for your puppy.

not like their teeth brushed regularly, or you may not be able to accomplish the task. In that case, you should consider a product that will help prevent plaque and calculus build-up.

The Plaque Attackers® and Galileo Bone® are other excellent choices for the first three years of a dog's life. Their shapes make them interesting for the dog. As the dog chews on them, the solid polyurethane massages the gums which improves the blood circulation to the periodontal tissues. Projections on the chew devices increase the surface and are in contact with the tooth for more efficient cleaning. The unique shape and consistency prevent your dog from exerting excessive force on his own teeth or from breaking off pieces of the bone. If your dog is an aggressive chewer or weighs more than 55 pounds (25 kg), you should consider giving him a Nylabone®, the most durable chew product on the market.

By the time dogs are four years old, 75% of them have periodontal disease. It is the most common infection in dogs. Yearly examinations by your veterinarian are essential to maintaining your dog's good health. If your veterinarian detects periodontal disease, he or she may recommend a prophylactic cleaning. To do a thorough cleaning, it will be necessary to put your dog under anesthesia. With modern gas anesthetics and monitoring equipment, the procedure is pretty safe. Your veterinarian will scale the teeth with an ultrasound scaler or hand instrument. This removes the calculus from the teeth. If there are calculus deposits below the gum line, the veterinarian will

Make sure you examine your Cavalier's mouth on a weekly basis for plaque and gum disease.

All dogs need safe chew toys to keep their teeth and jaws occupied.

Some veterinarians believe there is a correlation between unhealthy teeth and mitral valve disease, making it very important to have your Cavalier's teeth cleaned on a regular basis.

plane the roots to make them smooth. After all of the calculus has been removed, the teeth are polished with pumice in a polishing cup. If any medical or surgical treatment is needed, it is done at this time. The final step would be fluoride treatment and your follow-up treatment at home. If the periodontal disease is advanced, the veterinarian may prescribe a medicated mouth rinse or antibiotics for use at home. Make sure your dog has safe, clean and attractive chew toys and treats.

Rawhide is the most popular of all materials for a dog to chew. This has never been good news to dog owners, because rawhide is inherently very dangerous for dogs. Thousands of dogs have died from rawhide, having swallowed the hide after it has become soft and mushy, only to cause stomach and intestinal blockage. A new rawhide product on the market has finally solved the problem of rawhide: molded Roar-Hide® from Nylabone. These are composed of processed, cut up, and melted American rawhide injected into your dog's favorite shape: a dog bone. These dog-safe devices smell

Cavaliers live long, healthy lives with properly maintained teeth.

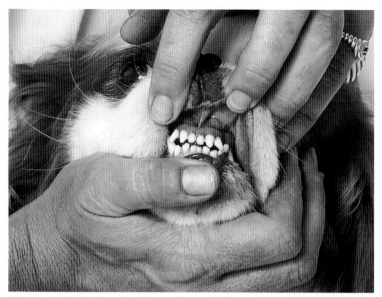

Check your Cavalier's teeth and mouth as part of his regular grooming routine.

and taste like rawhide but don't break up. The ridges on the bones help to fight tartar build-up on the teeth and they last ten times longer than the usual rawhide chews.

As your dog ages, professional examination and cleaning should become more frequent. The mouth should be inspected at least once a year. Your veterinarian may recommend visits every six months. In the geriatric patient, organs such as the heart, liver, and kidneys do not function as well as when they were young. Your veterinarian will probably want to test these organs' functions prior to using general anesthesia for dental cleaning. If your dog is a good chewer and you work closely with your veterinarian, your dog can keep all of its teeth all of its life. However, as your dog ages, his sense of smell, sight, and taste will diminish. He may not have the desire to chase, trap or chew his toys. He will also not have the energy to chew for long periods, as arthritis and periodontal disease make chewing painful. This will leave you with more responsibility for keeping his teeth clean and healthy. The dog that would not let you brush his teeth at one year of age, may let you brush his teeth now that he is ten years old.

If you train your dog with good chewing habits as a puppy, he will have healthier teeth throughout his life.

IDENTIFICATION and Finding the Lost Dog

There are several ways of identifying your dog. The old standby is a collar with dog license, rabies, and ID tags. Unfortunately collars have a way of being separated from the dog and tags fall off. We're not suggesting you shouldn't use a collar and tags. If they stay intact and on the dog, they are the quickest way of identification.

For several years owners have been tattooing their dogs. Some tattoos use a number with a registry. Here lies the problem because there are several registries to check. If you wish to tattoo, use your social security number. The humane shelters have the means to trace it. It is usually done on the inside of the rear thigh. The area is first shaved and numbed. There is no pain, although a few dogs do not like the buzzing sound. Occasionally tattooing is not legible and needs to be redone.

The newest method of identification is microchipping. The microchip is a computer chip that is no larger than a grain of rice. The veterinarian implants it by injection between the shoulder blades. The dog feels no discomfort. If your dog is lost and picked up by the humane society, they can trace you by scanning the microchip, which has its own code. Microchip

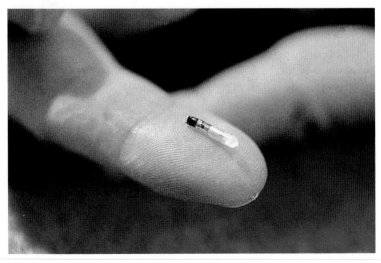

The newest method of identification is microchipping. The microchip is a computer chip that is no bigger than a grain of rice.

scanners are friendly to other brands of microchips and their registries. The microchip comes with a dog tag saying the dog is microchipped. It is the safest way of identifying your dog.

FINDING THE LOST DOG

I am sure you will agree that there would be little worse than losing your dog. Responsible pet owners rarely lose their dogs. They do not let their dogs run free because they don't want harm to come to them. Not only that but in most, if not all, states there is a leash law.

Beware of fenced-in yards. They can be a hazard. Dogs find ways to escape either over or under the fence. Another fast exit is through the gate that perhaps the neighbor's child left unlocked.

Below is a list that hopefully will be of help to you if you need it. Remember don't give up, keep looking. Your dog is worth your efforts.

1. Contact your neighbors and put flyers with a photo on it in their mailboxes. Information you should include would be the dog's name, breed, sex, color, age, source of identification, when your dog was last seen and where, and your name and phone numbers. It may be helpful to say the dog needs medical care. Offer a *reward*.

2. Check all local shelters daily. It is also possible for your dog to be picked up away from home and end up in an out-of-the-way shelter. Check these too. Go in person. It is not good enough to call. Most shelters are limited on the time they can hold dogs then they are put up for adoption or euthanized. There is the possibility that your dog will not make it to the shelter for several days. Your dog could have been wandering or someone may have tried to keep him.

3. Notify all local veterinarians. Call and send flyers.

4. Call your breeder. Frequently breeders are contacted when one of their breed is found.

5. Contact the rescue group for your breed.

6. Contact local schools—children may have seen your dog.

7. Post flyers at the schools, groceries, gas stations, convenience stores, veterinary clinics, groomers and any other place that will allow them.

8. Advertise in the newspaper.

9. Advertise on the radio.

TRAVELING with Your Dog

The earlier you start traveling with your new puppy or dog, the better. He needs to become accustomed to traveling. However, some dogs are nervous riders and become carsick easily. It is helpful if he starts with an empty stomach. Do not despair, as it will go better if you continue taking him with you on short fun rides. How would you feel if every time you rode in the car you stopped at the doctor's for an injection? You would soon dread that nasty car. Older dogs that tend to get carsick may have more of a problem adjusting to traveling. Those dogs that are having a serious problem may benefit from some medication prescribed by the veterinarian.

Do give your dog a chance to relieve himself before getting into the car. It is a good idea to be prepared for a clean up with a leash, paper towels, bag and terry cloth towel.

The safest place for your dog is in a fiberglass crate, although close confinement can promote carsickness in some dogs. If your dog is nervous you can try letting him ride on the seat next to you or in someone's lap.

An alternative to the crate would be to use a car harness made for dogs and/or a safety strap attached to the harness or collar. Whatever you do, do not let your dog ride in the back of a pickup truck unless he is securely tied on a very short lead. I've seen trucks stop quickly and, even though the dog was tied, it fell out and was dragged.

Another advantage of the crate is that it is a safe place to leave him if you need to run into the store. Otherwise you wouldn't be able to leave the windows down. Keep in mind that while many dogs are overly protective in their crates, this may not be enough to deter dognappers. In some states it is against the law to leave a dog in the car unattended.

Never leave a dog loose in the car wearing a collar and leash. More than one dog has killed himself by hanging. Do not let him put his head out an open window. Foreign debris can be blown into his eyes. When leaving your dog unattended in a car, consider the temperature. It can take less than five minutes to reach temperatures over 100 degrees Fahrenheit.

TRIPS

Perhaps you are taking a trip. Give consideration to what is best for your dog—traveling with you or boarding. When traveling by car, van or motor home, you need to think ahead about locking your vehicle. In all probability you have many valuables in the car and do not wish to leave it unlocked. Perhaps most valuable and not replaceable is your dog. Give thought to securing your vehicle and providing adequate ventilation for him. Another consideration for you when traveling with your dog is medical problems that may arise and little inconveniences, such as exposure to external parasites. Some areas of the country are quite flea infested. You may want to carry flea spray with you. This is even a good idea when staying in motels. Quite possibly you are not the only occupant of the room.

Unbelievably many motels and even hotels do allow canine guests, even some very first-class ones. Gaines Pet Foods Corporation publishes *Touring With Towser*, a directory of domestic hotels and motels that accommodate guests with dogs. Their address is Gaines TWT, PO Box 5700, Kankakee, IL, 60902. Call ahead to any motel that you may be considering and see if they accept pets. Sometimes it is necessary to pay a deposit against room damage. The management may feel reassured if you mention that your dog

Traveling with your Cavalier need not be a harrowing experience if he is properly crate-trained and comfortable riding in the car.

will be crated. If you do travel with your dog, take along plenty of baggies so that you can clean up after him. When we all do our share in cleaning up, we make it possible for motels to continue accepting our pets. As a matter of fact, you should practice cleaning up everywhere you take your dog.

Depending on where your are traveling, you may need an up-to-date health certificate issued by your veterinarian. It is good policy to take along your dog's medical information, which would include the name, address and phone number of your veterinarian, vaccination record, rabies certificate, and any medication he is taking.

AIR TRAVEL

When traveling by air, you need to contact the airlines to check their policy. Usually you have to make arrangements up to a couple of weeks in advance for traveling with your dog. The airlines require your dog to travel in an airline approved fiberglass crate. Usually these can be purchased through the airlines but they are also readily available in most pet-supply stores. If your dog is not accustomed to a crate, then it is a good idea to get him acclimated to it before your trip. The day of the actual trip you should withhold water about one hour ahead of departure and no food for about 12 hours. The airlines generally have temperature restrictions, which do not allow pets to travel if it is either too cold or too hot. Frequently these restrictions are based on the temperatures at the departure and arrival airports. It's best to inquire about a health certificate. These usually need to be issued within ten days of departure. You should arrange for non-stop, direct flights and if a commuter plane should be involved, check to see if it will carry dogs. Some don't. The Humane Society of the United States has put together a tip sheet

Family vacations can be very enjoyable when you bring your Cavalier along.

They're off and running! The Cavaliers' easygoing nature allows them to make themselves at home wherever they go.

for airline traveling. You can receive a copy by sending a self-addressed stamped envelope to:

The Humane Society of the United States
Tip Sheet
2100 L Street NW
Washington, DC 20037.

Regulations differ for traveling outside of the country and are sometimes changed without notice. Well in advance you need to write or call the appropriate consulate or agricultural department for instructions. Some countries have lengthy quarantines (six months), and countries differ in their rabies vaccination requirements. For instance, it may have to be given at least 30 days ahead of your departure.

Do make sure your dog is wearing proper identification including your name, phone number and city. You never know when you might be in an accident and separated from your dog. Or your dog could be frightened and somehow manage to escape and run away.

Another suggestion would be to carry in-case-of-emergency instructions. These would include the address and phone number of a relative or friend, your veterinarian's name, address and phone number, and your dog's medical information.

Boarding Kennels

Perhaps you have decided that you need to board your dog. Your veterinarian can recommend a good boarding facility or possibly a pet sitter that will come to your house. It is customary

What could be more fun than a Cavalier puppy? Four, of course!

for the boarding kennel to ask for proof of vaccination for the DHLPP, rabies and bordetella vaccine. The bordetella should have been given within six months of boarding. This is for your protection. If they do not ask for this proof I would not board at their kennel. Ask about flea control. Those dogs that suffer flea-bite allergy can get in trouble at a boarding kennel. Unfortunately boarding kennels are limited on how much they are able to do.

For more information on pet sitting, contact NAPPS:
National Association of Professional Pet Sitters
1200 G Street, NW
Suite 760
Washington, DC 20005.

Some pet clinics have technicians that pet sit and technicians that board clinic patients in their homes. This may be an alternative for you. Ask your veterinarian if they have an employee that can help you. There is a definite advantage of having a technician care for your dog, especially if your dog is on medication or is a senior citizen.

You can write for a copy of *Traveling With Your Pet* from ASPCA, Education Department, 441 E. 92nd Street, New York, NY 10128.

RESOURCES

American Cavalier King Charles Spaniel Club, Inc.
Secretary: Judith Gates
1540 Pawtucket Avenue
Rumford, RI 02916-1624
www.ACKCSC.org

American Kennel Club
260 Madison Avenue
New York, New York 10016
or 5580 Centerview Drive
Raleigh, North Carolina 27606
919-233-3600
919-233-9767
www.akc.org

The United Kennel Club, Inc.
100 E. Kilgore Road
Kalamazoo, Michigan 49002-5584
616-343-9020
www.ukcdogs.com

The Kennel Club
1 Clarges Street
Picadilly, London WIY 8AB, England

Canadian Kennel Club
Suite 100
89 Skyway Avenue
Etobicoke, Ontario, Canada M9W6R4

Index

Adolescence, 49
Age, 41
Aggression, 140
Agility, 98, 112
Air travel, 156
Alansmere Aquarius, 13
American Cavalier King Charles
    Spaniel Club, 15, 33
American Kennel Club, 33, 39,
    101, 115
Ann's Son, 10
Bathing, 75
Bell, Sally, 15
Boarding kennels, 157
Body language, 137
Bordetella, 121
Breeders, 30
Breeding, 25, 129
British Dogs, 10
Brown, Mrs. W. L. Lyons, 13
Campanozzi, Paula, 15
Canadian Kennel Club, 13, 101
Canine good citizen, 110
Car travel, 155
Cataracts, 32
Cavalier King Charles Club, 12
Cavalier King Charles Spaniel
    Club, USA, 13
*Cavalier King Charles Spaniel
    Today*, 9
Charles II, King, 9
Chewing, 144
Cheyletiella, 128
Coat care, 70
Coccidiosis, 125
Come command, 88
Conformation, 102-108
Coronavirus, 122
Crates, 80, 154
Dalziel, Hugh, 10
Demodectic mange, 128
Diet sheet, 45
Diet, 61, 65
—special, 65
Distemper, 119
Dog food, 62
*Dogs of Great Britain, America, and
    Other Countries, The*, 10
Down command, 92

Ear care, 74
Eldridge, Roswell, 10
England, 8
Evans, John, 13
Exercise, 67
Eye care, 75
Fear, 140
Feeding, 60
Fiennes, Richard and Alice, 6
Fleas, 127
Gammon, John, 15
Gender, 23
Giardiasis, 125
Gridley, Owen, 13
Hair dryers, 77
Hancock, Col. David, 7]
Health guarantee, 47
Heartworms, 126
Heel command, 95
Hepatitis, 120
Heritage of the Dog, The, 7
Hip dysplasia, 32
Hookworms, 124
Housetraining, 80-85
—crates, 80-85
Humane Society of the United
    States, 157
Hunting titles, 114
Identification papers, 42
Immunizations, 118
Inoculations, 42
Johnson-Snyder, Meredith, 15
Junior showmanship, 109
Kennel Club of Great Britain, 12,
    101
Kennel cough, 121
Leash training, 88
Leptospirosis, 120
Luxxar Deep Ellum, Ch., 15
Lyme disease, 122
Mange, 128
Marlborough, Duke of, 9
Mary, Queen of Scots, 9
Microchipping, 152
Mitral valve heart disease, 32
Nail trimming, 72
National Association of
    Professional Pet Sitters, 158
Natural History of Dogs, The, 6

Neutering, 25, 130
No command, 87
Nutrition, 60
Obedience, 110
Parasites, 124-128
—external, 127, 128
—internal, 124-126
Parvovirus, 120
Pedigree, 44
Performance tests, 114
Personality, 6
Puppy kindergarten, 101
Puppy, 34-41
—coat, 71
—health, 34, 36, 37
—selection, 34, 36
—show prospect, 37-41
Rabies, 121
Ravenrush Gillespie, Ch., 15
Registration certificate, 45
Retinal dysplasia, 32
Roundworms, 124
Sarcoptic mange, 128
Schroll, Robert, 15
Sit command, 90
Smith, Sheila, 9
Socialization, 47, 69, 135
Spaying, 25, 130
Stay command, 90
Stonehenge, 10
Supplementation, 64
Tapeworms, 125
Tattooing, 152
Temperament, 47
Therapy dog, 99
Ticks, 128
Tooth care, 74
Tracking, 112
Training classes, 96
Training, basic, 78, 85, 135
Veterinarian, 116, 123
—annual exam, 123
—first checkup, 116
—physical exam, 116
Water, 62
Weather concerns, 67-69
Whipworms, 124
Wye Rebound of Rattlebridge, 15
Yoder, Lamont, 15